The Top 2%

THE ULTIMATE GUIDE TO LANDING MORE CLIENTS, BOOSTING SALES AND BECOMING THE WORDPRESS HERO YOU WERE DESTINED TO BE...

David Papandreas

THE TOP 2%

THE ULTIMATE GUIDE TO LANDING MORE CLIENTS, BOOSTING SALES AND BECOMING THE WORDPRESS HERO YOU WERE DESTINED TO BE...

DAVID PAPANDREAS

****

www.WPDevHero.com

****

Earnings And Income Disclaimer

COPYRIGHT

ISBN: 9798324649234

Contents

This book is dedicated to my amazing wife, Liz, for always believing in me and giving me the encouragement and support to follow my dreams. And to my 2 wonderful children, Owen and Emily, for bringing so much joy and happiness into my life.

Introduction

The world is changing.

The internet has made the world smaller and has brought wonderful advances never before seen in history. It's also created more competition than ever before.

Now website owners can find developers to work on their sites anywhere in the world with only a few clicks of the mouse or taps on the smartphone.

If you're working as a freelance WordPress developer or considering it, you've probably realized that there is so much more to working with clients than just delivering quality code.

To be in the top 2% of freelance WordPress developers, you really need to know and understand how to effectively manage clients. This is something that can take years of trial and error and include many stressful, sometimes depressing days.

There are so many brilliant WordPress developers in the world, who understand the coding process, who can solve people's challenges and find creative solutions, but who struggle with the communication part of the business.

Make no mistake, being a freelance WordPress developer IS a business. It's a business where you wear all the hats. You're the Founder, CEO and Project Manager, so being able to effectively communicate with clients is imperative and is a skill you need to master. Otherwise, you run the risk of constantly being in a state of feast or famine and becoming over-worked and over-stressed so much so that you no longer enjoy what you're doing.

Since 2011, I've been helping people with their WordPress websites. Starting as a consultant talking to clients and business owners, I would take time to understand what challenges they were having and help them find solutions to their challenges. Then I would help them implement those solutions using WordPress.

My life took a dramatic turn when I joined Codeable in 2015 as the 4th team member in the company and the first support hire. In case you haven't heard of Codeable.io, it's the world's largest online marketplace for connecting the top 2% of vetted WordPress developers with clients around the world.

Over the next 4 years, I worked around the clock helping to support both clients and our developers, who we refer to as experts, and I personally resolved more than 41,263 conversations/support tickets in Intercom.

This experience gave me a unique insight into not only working alongside and helping our developers but also learning from them what works and what doesn't.

The developers at Codeable are all really quite amazing. It's a uniquely supportive, encouraging community where they really don't see each other as the "competition", but rather as colleagues, peers, and friends. And we do all we can as a company to foster this supportive environment, nurture it, and help it to continue to grow in the right direction.

After those first 4 years leading the support team, I transitioned to an Expert Advocate role in Codeable. Because of my years of experience and understanding what challenges developers face on a daily basis while working with clients, I was able to share this insight with our community to help them to reduce stress, earn more money, and have more fun while working.

I began to realize that while I'm helping our current community of developers, there is a worldwide community of freelance WordPress developers who could also benefit from my experience.

That's why I decided to write this book. To help other developers become better at managing clients and earning more money, all the while reducing stress, and enjoying the process more.

I honestly believe that you have what it takes to become a world-class freelance WordPress developer. Someone who embodies what I think of as a WP Dev Hero. And I want to help you become the hero you were destined to be.

While reading through the chapters, feel free to skip around and pick/choose what interests you the most.

I refer to this as cafeteria-style learning. Picking and choosing which topics to learn about.

Maybe you already have a great system for finding clients to work with and you don't need any extra help in this area. If that's the case, then fantastic and I'm genuinely happy for you as I know this can be a cause of stress and anxiety for many other developers. For those developers who ARE looking for ways to find more clients to work with, then this chapter will interest you a great deal and you'll find it very helpful.

Maybe you already have a system in place to reduce scope creep and this isn't an issue for you. If so, again that's wonderful and feel free to skip over this section. If you struggle with this aspect of the business, then I highly encourage you to spend time here to learn how to effectively reduce and even prevent scope creep.

So jump around in the book to find the chapter that interests you the most, and dive in!

I've purposely kept chapters as short as possible so that it wasn't filled with a lot of fluff and instead it gets straight to the point as quickly as possible. I didn't want you to have to read a 400-page novel that might take 3 months to finish. You could probably read this book cover to cover in just a couple of hours.

The idea with this book was to pick out the topics I felt were most important and that would have the largest impact for freelance WordPress developers. I want to give you the ideas, concepts, and strategies that I've learned while working with some of the best WordPress developers in the world at Codeable, and share them with you here in this easy to read and digest book.

If you're ready to elevate your journey as a freelance WordPress developer, I invite you to join the Freelance Dev Hero tribe on Skool.

This is more than just a community; it's a transformational experience where I will personally guide and support you, alongside like-minded professionals who are all striving to be the best of the best.

Together, we will tackle the real challenges of client management, scope creep, and more, equipping you with the tools to thrive and enjoy the rewards of being a top freelance WordPress developer.

Don't just read about success—live it.

Join us now at Skool.com/freelance-dev-hero and step into the role of the hero you were destined to be.

Let's grow, succeed, and lead the field, together.

Chapter One

Where To Find Clients

Needing fresh, new clients is part of what can make working as a freelance developer so stressful. Especially when you're getting started and before you have a number of happy repeat clients. Even after having a large pool of past happy clients, some developers consistently struggle to find new paying clients to keep the projects and revenue coming in.

The question I get asked most by WP developers is where to find great clients. There are so many places to find people who need website help and I'll review a handful of different options to consider in your search. But I also want you to be aware that once you get started on this path and after you've worked with a client, don't just do the service for them and leave to find the next client.

There's an entire strategy of maximizing your revenue per client and per project so that you don't leave money on the table while you provide maximum value and care to your client. We cover that in more detail in Chapter 12 Up-Sells, but I just want you to be aware that once you start finding clients to work with, you'll get to a point where you don't need to always be searching for the next client and you'll want to grow and nurture the relationships you already have so that they keep coming back to you and paying you over and over and over again.

Now let's focus now on finding clients, whether it's your very first client or simply the next client that you can work with.

So what are some options to consider?

One option is to look to online marketplaces like UpWork, Freelancer, or Guru.

While there are a large number of projects being posted on these marketplace websites, beware as it can be challenging to cut through the clutter and the large number of "Bids" a client is receiving.

UpWork actually prides itself on the fact that a client will receive 60-80 bids on their project. While this may sound "nice" to a client up-front, the reality is it often becomes overwhelming to clients to try and find the right developer for their project and it can become daunting for a developer to try and cut through all this noise.

It's also hard when clients are receiving so many bids (many of them quite low in price), that they can become conditioned to expecting very low prices to get work done, thereby devaluing your services and your time.

That said, there are freelance developers who do quite well on these marketplaces and you can find some great clients to work with. For more detailed help on being effective on UpWork and similar marketplaces, Victor(ious) has a blog post I recommend checking out titled, "Guide: How I Made $7,645 Part-time On UpWork in Less than 2 Months"

You may also consider looking on forums like Craigslist or Reddit for people requesting help.

When using Reddit, I'll suggest specifically heading to the **/r/forhire** subreddit and then searching at the top for "**WordPress**". Do exercise a bit of caution as people here are often looking for very low prices to complete their requests and sometimes the clients looking to pay the least often expect the most and can be demanding. But it's still possible to find some good clients and nice projects on these sites, so don't write them off completely. And when using a site like Craigslist, make sure to check other cities and not just your own city, especially if you live in a smaller population area where fewer requests might be posted.

Another option is to consider applying to Codeab le.io

There is a very thorough vetting process that you must pass, where only the top 2% of WordPress developers who apply end up making it through to become an Expert on the platform. But if you make it through the process, the rewards are a guaranteed hourly rate of $70–120 USD, a steady stream of new projects from nice clients who understand your value, and being a part of a global community of other WordPress developers who are some of the nicest people you'll ever meet.

A more advanced strategy is to take to social media. There are 2 specific methods; one involves using Facebook (or LinkedIn) and "infiltrating" Groups, and the other method is to turn on your camera and press record.

When turning to Facebook (or LinkedIn as the strategy is the same for both), to find prospects and clients, there is a specific strategy that I'm referring to. This involves setting up your personal profile in a business-minded way, versus your personal family-life way as most people do.

This includes using a professional looking profile photo of yourself (not your pet, not you at the beach, and not you making "silly" faces). Then upload a cover photo that has been edited in Photoshop or Canva to include what you specialize in and how to reach you. For example, including links to your other social media accounts or podcast...

You'll also want to make some posts in your timeline that show your knowledge and offers specific helpful information for accomplishing different things using WordPress. As an example, you might post a helpful guide to optimizing images, how to speed up your WordPress site, or anything else you can think of to provide value and helpful information for people. Keep it short, actionable, and only a small specific task. Meaning don't go into a complex coding project that loses the person after the first 2 minutes.

If you'd like to check out a perfect example of this profile in action, have a look at Julie Stoian's profile below. At the time of writing this, she had a beautiful, high-converting Facebook profile that elegantly displays these principles. Just in case, I've included a screenshot of it below:

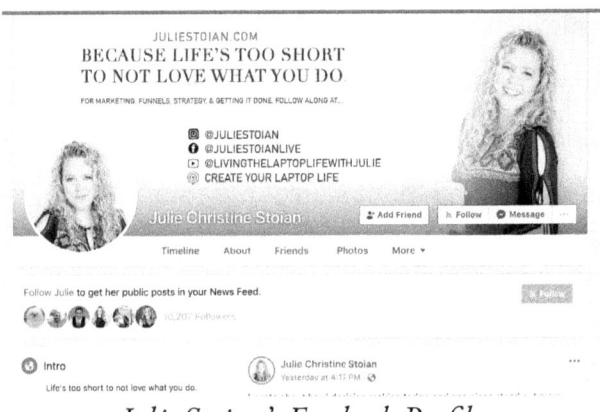

Julie Stoian's Facebook Profile

Once you have your Facebook profile looking professional, and your few helpful content pieces loaded into your timeline, you'll then start going into different Facebook (or LinkedIn) Groups with the sole-intention of looking for people you can help.

These Groups might be WordPress related, entrepreneur related, startup related, e-commerce, or local business related. Join these different groups and begin scrolling through the posts made by other users and find people asking questions that you feel you can help.

To give you a few example FB Groups to help get you started, I'll suggest checking out and joining:

1. Freedom Hackers Mastermind - 48k members

2. Freedom to Freelance Project - 5,500 members

3. Entrepreneur Hustle - 48k members

4. Rising Tide Society - 76k members

These are a few good LinkedIn Groups to consider joining, among others:

1. A Startup Specialists Group - 284k members

2. Band of Entrepreneurs - 27k members

3. Bright Ideas & Entrepreneurs - 22k member

4. Digital Marketing – 1.1m members

Please **DO NOT** spam your contact information or make posts about working with you. This won't lead to anything meaningful and will likely get you ejected from the group really quickly and permanently banned.

Instead, take time to write a detailed and thorough reply to the person asking the question, and make it genuinely helpful. This will not only get the attention of the person who asked the question, but many other people who read your reply.

When people see your reply, they'll think, *Wow, this person really knows what they're talking about* and they'll naturally click on your name to check out who you are and visit your profile. This is where they'll see your nice photo, your professional cover photo, your helpful detailed posts in your timeline, and will naturally message you asking for your help or clicking over to your website to want to learn more about you and reach out to work with you.

I know a freelancer who used this exact strategy to earn 6-figures in her first year. It works if you're willing to work it.

This same strategy can be used over on Quora as well. Taking time to leave detailed, thoughtful, genuinely helpful replies to people's questions, which will naturally cause them to want to learn more about you, click over to your website, and want to do business with you.

The other Facebook strategy is to start doing regular Facebook Live's. These are best done with your smartphone to record yourself as they're very natural and you don't need to worry about being fancy or having a super polished script. Simply press record and start delivering value. This value will be in the form of helping people with a different aspect of their WordPress site.

Again, the video could be about how to speed up a WordPress site. Or it could be about how to make sure their plugins, theme, and WP core are kept up-to-date to prevent security vulnerabilities. Or you can talk about where to find great royalty-free images to use in their posts (i.e. Pixabay or Unsplash). There are so many things you could help WordPress website owners with and the more often you do these Facebook Lives, the more reach you'll end up receiving.

If you're thinking to yourself, *well that's great, but I only have a few friends and family members associated with my profile*, that's totally ok and don't let this stop you from getting started. This strategy works even if you don't have *any* friends or followers on Facebook and are starting from 0. The more you post Facebook Live videos, the more reach Facebook will start generating for you... Zuckerberg *loves* content and just start posting. The more you post the better your videos will become over time.

While recording your video, <u>be sure to mention how to get in touch with you, and that you can help them with this topic</u> you're speaking about. This is like your mini-sales pitch, without seeming like a used-car salesman.

You're providing real value, helping to teach something, and then offering additional help to those who need it. It's best to mention how people can get in touch with you at least 2x in your video; once in the middle and again at the end of the video. And after the video, you can add your website link to the description or comments. For a reasonable monthly fee, there are some apps you can use that will allow you to add text overlays to your live Facebook Live videos as well, such as Be.Live.

Then after you've done 15-25 of these Facebook Lives, you can check your stats to see which videos got the most engagement and then consider putting $10 into Facebook Ads to boost those videos to an even wider audience.

You can also take those videos after they're done and download them to your computer to then upload them to your YouTube channel to get even more traffic and organic reach.

Another option to consider, and how I personally got my first few clients, is looking to your community, your friends, your family, your family's friends, or your neighbors. I can almost guarantee there is someone very close in proximity to you right now who is needing help with their website. I'll go into my personal story of how I unexpectedly came across my very first client towards the end of this chapter... And when you meet someone new, hand them your business card.

Important: Make sure to also get business cards of everyone you meet and actually follow up with them. Some people will go to an event. Fewer people hand out their business cards. Fewer people still get other people's business cards. And even fewer ever follow-up. The money is hiding in the follow-up.

You might also consider hosting your own events for local businesses in your area where people can come together to network. You can share ideas and strategies with the group, and when they need help implementing them, who do you think they'll turn to?

By organizing an event (which is easier than you think), you become the trusted advisor and the one people will want to work with after you've demonstrated your knowledge and expertise with the group.

There are lots of people online who have trust issues with other people they've only ever "met" online. They don't know you and they don't know where you live geographically. This means they never really know who they will be working with or if their project will get done. After all, they might pay someone for help and the person then disappears with their money never to be seen again.

It's surprising how many developers and development agency websites act like big companies, use stock photos, list generic services, and don't reveal any personal information or even a picture of themselves or their team. This impersonal experience can be challenging for a client to overcome when looking to hire a developer to work on their website.

This is made worse if the website owner (who is requesting help) is generating revenue from their site. It's like finding some random person you just met off the street and asking them to clean your office, after-hours, when nobody is there. *Take my keys, let yourself in, clean everything, but please don't rob me.*

Many of these trust issues can be alleviated and overcome when a person can meet you face-to-face, which is why I love the personal connection you get from meeting new people *in-person*.

They can see your smile, hear you speak, listen to the helpful advice you're sharing, the insightful questions you're asking, and how you talk about different aspects of web development, so they know you're the real deal. If you can communicate your passion of WordPress and helping people, you'll be unforgettable in the minds of those you meet.

If you're not able to connect with someone face-to-face in person, then the next best thing is a call (preferably video, but audio-only is great too).

Another effective strategy to build trust is to showcase testimonials from satisfied clients. Include links to reviews or even text-only endorsements describing the quality of your work. Always obtain permission from the individuals before using their testimonials. For added credibility, accompany each review with the person's full name and location. This approach is far more convincing than simply using a first name and a generic stock photo.

I'm a big believer in that people want to do business with people they **know, like, and trust.** Finding people exclusively online can make this process slightly more challenging because you might be living in another city, another state, or even another country. At this point, you're wanting someone who's never met you, doesn't know if you are who you say you are, doesn't know if you'll steal their money and not do the service, or that you won't break their website leaving them in an even worse position than when they started.

So how do you get someone to know you, like you, and trust you?

I truly believe the fastest way to accomplish this is by meeting people in person. If someone can meet you in person, they have a chance to talk with you and get to know you. You're able to answer their questions and help them feel comfortable by displaying your knowledge and comprehension around not only websites but in solving their specific challenges.

Again, whether that's building them a website, fixing their website problem, or adding a new feature to their website that helps them accomplish their goals, they'll get to know you better and trust you more.

Your willingness to help them, talk with them, and share information with them will result in them liking you more.

Your knowledge and expertise of what you've shared with them will cause them to trust you so they think, *'This person really understands what I need and I feel comfortable giving them money in exchange for working on my website.'*

As a quick disclaimer, it's important to be cautious about how much you disclose. Share your knowledge regarding WHAT you'll do for your clients, but avoid delving into the specifics of HOW you'll achieve it. This approach helps protect your trade secrets and prevents potential clients from attempting to DIY the solutions after consulting with you. Always remember to focus on the WHAT, not the HOW.

In the end, it all comes down to relationships.

Let's get into some specifics about how to interact with people, face to face, to establish trust and authority...

When you meet new people, strike up conversations with them. Talk about *their* business and *their* website. Ask *them* questions and take a *genuine* interest in what they have going on. You might also ask them where they are from in the hopes it's someplace you've also been or are also from; this helps to create a faster bond with you when you can find common-ground. You might be surprised how many people have been to, used to live in, or know someone from your same town.

Heck, you may be able to find some things in common by checking out your potential client's website! I know of developers in the Top 2% who have created super bonds with some of their clients over their content on their site, their store, or even their site's mission that really resonates with them.

Then in the course of the conversation, the other person will be feeling so good talking about themselves that they'll finally start asking questions about *you* and what you do. This is when you can really shine!

Let them know how you're a WordPress developer and how you help clients to achieve their goals, make their life easier, and reduce their stress and frustration with their websites.

Consider talking specifically about how many of your clients don't realize that their out-of-date plug-ins, theme and core can result in security vulnerabilities and hacked sites, which compromise their client's data, disrupt their business and cash flow, and result in much more costly work to clean up and re-secure.

Then you can transition into asking the client about their own site and if they know if everything is kept up-to-date and routinely checked?

98% of everyone you ask will say either "No" or "I Have No Idea"... this is when you can offer your services.

Offer to check their site for free and provide a free no obligation estimate for them to make sure everything is safely updated and secure. Most people will gladly take you up on this offer, and this is your "in". Remember to go the extra mile on their first project with you. This is one of the secrets to keeping clients long-term and getting them to refer you to their friends later.

During these face-to-face conversations, at some point, you'll probably find yourself pulling out your business card.

This can be a critical moment—within just a couple of seconds of receiving your card, a potential client will feel it, look it over, and then slip it into their pocket. First impressions matter, and you wouldn't want something like a piece of spinach stuck in your teeth to ruin it.

Likewise, you don't want to hand out a business card printed on flimsy cardstock or from your home printer, with the same old information everyone else uses.

For example, listing your services; Web Design, Web Development, WordPress, WooCommerce... or worse, only listing your Name, Company Name, Logo, Website URL, and Email Address.

This is super boring, provides no real value to this new potential client, and gives them no reason to contact you. They can look in the phonebook or on

Google and find 200 other local website developers in their town that all offer the same basic services.

You want your business card to make an impact, to really create that WOW factor. When someone first sees and touches your card, they should immediately notice the quality—the substantial weight and thickness, the smooth rounded corners. It looks and feels different from any other business card I've ever seen. And in my experience, nobody does this better than Moo.

Their line of LUXE business cards are simply phenomenal.

I personally recommend going for the LUXE line, in standard size so it fits comfortably in a wallet, with rounded corners and a choice of color for the middle layer. These business cards are essentially three layers thick, with two white outer cards for your information and a colored middle layer that adds a distinctive edge.

These cards stand out as superior in every way, and whenever I hand one out, I see the person's expression change to one of surprise and excitement. They often say, *'Oh wow, this is a really nice business card!*

Next comes what to place on your front AND back of your card to get this new potential client thinking *YES, I want to work with this person.*

You need to speak to your potential client in a language they can understand, with copy that speaks to them and their desires.

The front might include a compelling headline, a personal quote stating your guarantee, a professional looking photo of yourself, your name, business name, title, and any awards, certificates or recognition you've earned.

Then the back of your business card might include details about your guarantee, your call to action, your logo and contact information, and any trust badges (like awards, certifications, etc.), and lastly the payment options that you accept.

I've noticed a lot of WordPress developers looking for a business card that really speaks to the freelance lifestyle. So, I went ahead and created a custom business card template (.psd) for freelance WordPress developers, featuring both front and back designs.

You can grab this template over in the Free-lance Dev Hero Tribe on www.skool.com/free-lance-dev-hero

It's a place where I personally help and guide WordPress developers on their path to becoming the best of the best. Join us, and the template is yours for free. Let's grow together.

If you look on fiverr, you may find lots of different business card formats that are flashy and bright. But you don't need a flashy card with lots of design work, colors and full of platitudes, like *"Work With The Best!"* or *"I'm The Developer For You!"* Or even worse, generic cookie-cutter cards that look like every other developer or agency stock cards listing your services.

You want a business card that gets your phone to ring or causes people to email you with requests for work they want done. And the business card format I described above does just that.

After you've worked with a client on their project, and they've had a great experience and are happy with your work, I'll suggest sending them a quick handwritten Thank You card in the mail (real mail, NOT email).

Something quick and easy to say thank you to the client for trusting you with their website development and that you were glad to have been able to help them. Then in the P.S. line, after your signature, say *"By the way, I've included 3 business cards for you and if you might have any friends that need WordPress development done, I'll be honored if you'll think of me. And if you'll tell your friend to mention your name when they contact me, I'll be happy to give them a $50 discount on any service they need done, and also give you a $50 discount on any future work you may need. Thanks again!"*

This way your friend is being rewarded and their friend is rewarded and has extra incentive to work with you.

There's nothing more powerful than referrals! Especially when it's a referral from a friend. This is also why going the extra mile initially with a new client is a very good idea. There's never any traffic on the extra mile.

It's also VERY important to make sure to get your new friend's business card or contact information. In case they don't contact you, proceed with an offensive play. Meaning, take a few minutes to check out their website and then make solid recommendations.

Take note of their page load times (offer a speed optimization and what the benefits are), look to see if they're using an SSL (offer to secure their website using SSL and what the benefits are), look if they're collecting visitor's contact information (offer to set up a lead capture tool and what the benefits are), does their site look dated and old (offer a site redesign), etc.

Then when you reach out to them, you'll have some different options to recommend based on your findings. This will have a much bigger impact than simply contacting them asking if they'd like you to do anything on their website.

Now back to finding clients and where I found my first client...

The first client I got to work with me was a friend in my neighborhood. If you have a dog or a child this makes it even easier.

In my case, I had my son who was around 3 years old at the time, and after working my regular 9-5, I'd get home and take him outside to play. We would always run into the same couple of kids also playing in the neighborhood cul-de-sac and the dads would all be outside watching the kids play and be talking.

Since I'm passionate about websites and marketing, I would start talking to one dad in particular who I seemed to connect with the best. After learning he owned a local restaurant I googled it and found his website. I'd look it over, checking out each page, and start making mental notes about things I felt could be improved.

For example, he didn't have any type of online ordering. He wasn't capturing any contact information of visitors. His site looked old and outdated. He wasn't even using WordPress and was instead using a basic HTML coded site that he had no way of easily updating himself. And of course he wasn't using an SSL certificate... So I would start asking him questions about have you considered doing this? Have you thought about doing that? Do you know what SSL is and why it's important?

After a couple of weeks of this he finally told me, *"You really know a lot about websites, do you think you could help me with some of the things we've been talking about?"*

I, of course, said, *"Sure, I'll be happy to!"*

We started with a new WP website with SSL. Then added a way to collect visitor's contact information in exchange for a small coupon. Then we added an online ordering option. Then we added an online store so he could ship his food (bagels in this case) across the country. Next we added a wholesale landing page so he could collect contact info of potential new distributors and I helped him set up Google AdWords campaigns to drive traffic to it.

He then asked if I could help him on a monthly basis to create and send new promo emails to everyone on his email list, so I set him up on a monthly retainer which lasted over 2 years.

If you'll start talking with your neighbors, I bet you'll discover there are people very close to you that would benefit from working with you as well.

Another place to find clients is by joining networking groups, your local Chamber of Commerce (if you live in the USA), Toastmasters International (which is worldwide), local Meetups (both for WordPress specific Meetups and Career & Business Meetups, and any other topic that interests you. Expat communities are a great networking opportunity as well, in case you're living in a different country than where you were born/raised. There is an instant connection in these communities since you all share that commonality of being from the same country. The more people you network with, meet, and get to know, the more people you'll find who have a genuine need for your services.

And when you meet these people, **DO NOT** talk about yourself first! I can't stress this enough - this is the secret sauce you've been looking for!

People care infinitely more about themselves than about YOU. So don't blurt out all about how you're a website developer and all of the great skillsets you have.

You need to try and focus the conversation 100% about them. Get them talking about themselves, ask lots of questions, take a genuine interest in them and act like you're their best friend (in a not creepy kind of way). And soon hopefully you will be their best friend if you take a genuine interest in them and go into it being a friend.

Don't worry, there will come a point when the other person starts asking YOU questions and wanting to learn more about you...

Don't be offended if the conversation doesn't come around to you until your 2nd or even 3rd encounter either. It probably will in the first chat, but if it doesn't then don't force it and be patient.

When the conversation does point back to you, and the other person starts asking you questions, that's when you can start talking about what you do, all the people and business you've helped, HOW you've helped them, and then you can start giving them ideas and feedback about their own website.

You might say things like *"I noticed on your website you're currently doing this, have you thought about doing that?"* Or *"I noticed when I was checking out your website that it was taking a really long time to load... have you noticed that as well? This is actually one of my specialties which is speeding up a website. Is that something you might be interested in? I'd love to help you with it since every additional second your website takes to load is causing visitors to abandon your site..."*

So not only tell them WHO you are, WHAT you do, and HOW you can help them but then let them know WHY this is important to them.

What does a slow loading website mean for them? What does an outdated (insecure) website mean to them and why should they care about that?

Telling someone you can speed up their website might interest a few people. But if you can help them understand why this is important, how it's costing them sales and lost revenue, they'll be interested to hear more.

And if they're spending money on PPC, how having a slow loading website is costing them extra money for paying for clicks but then the visitor clicks Back before their website actually loads and is wasting their ad-spend... then the person you're talking to will really start listening to you and taking your advice seriously and ASKING for your help. After all, nobody wants to waste money on ads.

When you do it this way and follow this process, you won't have to chase new clients and try to "sell" them on your services. They'll be asking to work with you and wanting to give you their money.

Now that you're finding and talking to people, let's build up the rapport even further. Remember, a sale is a process, not an event.

Chapter Two

Engaging With New Prospective Clients

(Building Up Your Rapport)

It's important when you're engaging with clients (especially new or prospective clients) to come across as the professional that you are. You want to look and act the part. That means conducting yourself like a professional. Dressing like a professional. Shaking hands like a professional.

This involves using proper grammar, spelling and communicating clearly with your clients. With existing clients, it's not as vital, because they already have a relationship with you. They already trust you and know you deliver great work. But these first and early impressions matter more than you think.

Please don't misunderstand, it's still important and don't get lazy in your communication because you can lose the trust and confidence in your client if your communication is riddled with errors, misspelled words, and grammatical errors.

Clients may think if you're sloppy with your written words, you may be getting sloppy with your code (even though we both know that's not the case and I know some brilliant coders who can't put sentences together to save their life!)

I highly recommend Grammarly.com or a free option called Languagetool.com to check your written communication in real time. And now with the advent of AI tools like ChatGPT, Gemini, and Claude, you can easily craft beautiful sentences that always sound professional. (Just make sure to read the output before pasting it across to your client; it may need a couple of tweaks before it's ready to send.)

Simply put, **always** re-read your messages before clicking send. This can ensure your communications with the client are always looking and reading great.

Pro-tip: when sending an email, do not enter the email address of the recipient until you've finished your message AND have re-read it at least 1x. This will help to prevent an accidental sending before you've had a chance to proof it.

When you're messaging a client and the content includes typos and grammar mistakes, it makes you come across as sloppy and an amateur. True professionals communicate well and don't include these mistakes.

If you're ready to join the Top 2% and become a WP Dev Hero, then it starts with your communication. This also helps you to command higher rates and you'll often have the luxury of turning clients away that you're not interested in working with.

I also highly recommend greeting the client properly and thanking them for taking the time to send you the details of their request or for explaining their request in such great detail.

You want to always be polite and friendly and come across as helpful and appreciative.

It doesn't need to be long and drawn-out, but a quick *'Thanks for reaching out and providing this new request. I appreciate the detail you put into it and would like to ask a few more questions to make sure I'm understanding everything...'*

Remember, people want to work with other people who they **Know**, **Like**, and **Trust**. Your LinkedIn profile or website will help them get to know you better, and like I discuss later in Chapter 15 on Manufacturing Celebrity, there are ways to build up your credibility and authority status so that they know you better, like you faster, and trust you more.

Think about how often you've done business with someone you didn't like...

I'm willing to bet that it's either never or very seldom, and only if they were your only option. But in today's environment, that's rarely the case and people have many choices with whom to do business with and exchange their money for services needed. So be likable. And people like people who are like themselves.

I suggest reading a book, watching some YouTube videos, or taking a class on NLP or Neurolinguistic Programming. It's not mind-control, but it's about as close as you can get. Specifically, there are techniques called <u>Matching and Mirroring</u> that can help you to model your style of communication based on the client to more closely resemble them. This is the foundation of building rapport, and doing so in the least amount of time.

Allow me to give you an example; if the client is very serious, direct, and to the point, then you should also be serious, direct and to the point. This means don't use smiley-face emojis if the client doesn't. Don't use "!" exclamation points if the client doesn't. If they don't communicate about the weather and "How're you today?" then you shouldn't either.

Some clients see this chit-chat as wasting time and they aren't asking you these things and so they don't want to read about you asking them. Stick to the facts, discuss the scope of work, ask questions related to their request, but keep it direct and to the point.

On the other hand, if the client is chatty, uses lots of emojis, likes to chat about the weather and pretty sunsets, then you should reply in-kind. This helps to show the client you're serious and you know your stuff by asking great questions about their project, but also that you're friendly and personable and have a happy demeanor. You just need to look at how the client is communicating and then match their style of communication.

The same applies in-person, face to face encounters. Pay attention to things like how they dress. How they shake your hand. How fast (or slow) they speak. Try to match it all (or as much as possible).

Before you think that this is manipulating someone, take a moment to stop and think about your best friends...

Don't you do this with them already?

Are there some friends that you plan to see and you know they'll be wearing a t-shirt and jeans, so you decide to wear a t-shirt and jeans?

Or who maybe talk loud, so when you're with them you also talk a bit louder than you normally do?

Or maybe you have a certain way you shake their hand or greet them when you see them?

There's really no difference here, other than you're speeding up the process of becoming their good friend to build this rapport. Why wait months or even years to start doing this when you can do it right off the bat from your first interactions with them. And I should hope you will become great friends with them and not solely try to manipulate the situation.

So after matching and mirroring the client (AKA your new friend), this will help to establish likability with them quickly. But how do you get them to trust you?

You may be someone they've never met in real life and you're asking them to give you money, and also hand over credentials to their website, which in some cases is a very valuable and precious thing. After all, their website may be their sole source of income. To use another similar example as before, it's like calling a refrigerator repair-person and giving them the keys to your house saying let yourself in, fix my refrigerator, and I'm trusting you not to steal anything while you're there.

How you develop trust is by establishing yourself as the professional, the doctor, the problem solver, who is here to save them.

And you do this by being friendly, thanking them for informing you of their project and explaining the issue they're having or wanting to be resolved, and you asking great questions to better define their request.

By asking great questions, it shows the client you know what you're talking about. It also helps the client think through their project request in even greater detail so that they get the impression of *"I thought I knew my project and what I wanted, but this developer is asking such fantastic questions that it's causing me to think through things I hadn't even considered... this person really knows their stuff and I feel really comfortable trusting them to complete my request."*

So what kinds of questions do you ask?

Don't confuse great questions with highly technical questions. I'm sure you've realized many clients aren't the most technical people (otherwise they wouldn't be coming to you). But they do need to get a sense that you know what you're talking about and that you're taking the time to understand their project requirements. As an added benefit, this also helps to further clarify and define the scope of work that's to be included, helps you provide a more accurate quote AND helps to prevent scope creep which we'll discuss a bit later in Chapter 9, How To Reduce And Even Prevent Scope Creep.

To illustrate this further, here's an example of a "Bad" question:

> *Will it be OK to use Beaver Builder to code your design?*

And here's an example of a "Good" question to ask:

> *I would like to use a page builder to code your design as it will give you the flexibility to do small edits and updates yourself in the future, and it will speed up the coding process so it'll ultimately cost you less money.*

> *Based on my experience, I would recommend Beaver Builder, as it's very easy to use, it's updated frequently, they have great support, and your page won't be built using short-codes. Beaver Builder instead outputs real HTML code for the page, so if you decide in the future you'd like to change themes, it'll be much easier to make this*

change and you won't be locked into using it forever or needing to rebuild each page from scratch.

Does that sound good to you, or do you have another preference?

Can you feel the difference in this?

Yes, you'll invest an additional 1-2 minutes in crafting your message to the client, but this provides more value to the client, helps them to understand why you're making this recommendation, and speaks to the client's concern of wanting to make their own updates and spend less money. Even if they don't come right out and say the words *"I want to make my own updates and spend less money,"* you can be sure it's in the back of their mind.

Now that we're building up your rapport with the client, lets increase your conversions to paid projects...

Chapter Three

Increasing Your Conversions To Paid Projects

How do you land more projects? By communicating well with clients pre-hire and asking lots of great questions.

When you no longer try "selling yourself" to clients on working with you and instead focus the conversation on helping the client, amazing things start to happen.

It's the craziest thing, if you genuinely take an interest in the client and their request, ask great questions to make sure you understand what they're wanting to have completed, you'll inevitably build up the relationship in the process. Then you're helping your client picture themselves going from a state of uncertainty, to seeing the finish line and how this can transform their business and they'll be in a state of relief (dare I say joy).

It can be easy and tempting to rush into a project. You're excited to be landing it and maybe even a little desperate to collect the money so you can pay some bills or buy some new tech. But this can lead to bigger problems like scope creep down the road or having to invest much more time into the project than you quoted or charged for. It's also not doing a service to the client to rush into it and you risk devaluing yourself and your craft.

What if the scope of work the client requested is crystal clear?

Then at the very least, re-state the scope of work letting the client know you fully understand what's needed and then asking the client to confirm you have understood their request properly and verify they have no other questions or concerns before getting started.

Most of the time though, there are questions that can be asked. Maybe it's just confirming that they have and will be able to provide access to the WP Admin, FTP, and/or hosting account.

You might be surprised to learn that some clients don't have this access, don't know where this access is or how to supply it, or aren't able to grant this access to you.

Knowing this upfront will help you to understand the requirements, confirm your ability to complete their request, and how much to charge if you'll need to be walking the client through these types of basic requests (i.e. how much hand-holding might be involved in this project).

You may also wish to help the client with creating User Stories for their requests as I detail in Chapter 9 on How To Reduce And Event Prevent Scope Creep. Not only can this help to reduce and in many cases eliminate scope creep, but it also adds value to the client and helps to ensure they receive precisely what they want.

Sometimes clients really don't know what they want... they THINK they know, but that's not always the case. Sometimes after you deliver their request, they realize this solution really doesn't solve their needs and they'll ask for revisions and additional work to be done.

You and I both know this is scope creep and additional work being requested, but clients only think of themselves and in their mind their issue isn't fully resolved. After all, they may have paid for a solution, not just your time.

I've heard from senior developers working at Word-Press VIP agencies that these agencies incorporate User Stories into every single project they work on. These senior developers then took this same approach to their freelancing work and include User Stories on everything they work on, even the smallest requests.

Everything includes a User Story and as a result, clients are consistently happy with the results and there's very little scope creep possible. If the new client request doesn't fit inside of the User Story, it's much easier to push back on it and request additional money for this additional work. We'll go into more detail on User Stories a bit later...

When thinking about the deadline to promise a client, it's always a great idea to under-promise and over-deliver. Meaning if you think you can complete a project by Wednesday, tell the client you'll have it delivered by Friday. Then still try your best to deliver it by Wednesday, so that if you run into any issues or challenges along the way, you'll have additional time built in and hopefully won't risk missing the agreed upon deadline.

If you happen to deliver it early, before Friday, then you look like a Hero instead of someone who can't keep their promises. And when you deliver early, they'll leave with such a wonderful experience that they'll go out of their way to work with you again to receive another wonderful experience.

What happens if it looks like you'll miss the deadline that was agreed to with the client? How early should you inform the client?

Answer: **As soon as possible.**

Never wait until the deadline or even the day before. Inform the client of any challenges that you are experiencing and if it looks like the deadline may not happen. This will allow the client to make accommodations on their end to account for this delay.

I've had developers tell me that when they communicate the issue(s) with the client, that the client really responds positively, especially when they are told what those issues are. This helps the client understand the situation better and gives them additional peace of mind knowing you aren't missing the deadline because you've been watching videos on YouTube instead of working on their project.

Also, consider asking the client if there is a specific feature or MVP (Minimum Viable Product) that might be needed as you may be able to shift your focus to complete just that portion of the project by the original deadline. Or if it would be ok to push the entire deadline back.

By giving the clients this small bit of control it can make a world of difference.

They can then decide for themselves what would be best to have and it might really save the day to have a specific feature implemented by the original deadline. For example, perhaps they have a launch scheduled for that day and by focusing on a specific feature, it won't delay their launch.

Or they may say that it's ok and if you can have the entire project delivered by the new deadline, then that will be fine.

But don't make this assumption or decision for them––it's always best to ask the client.

You might also consider informing the client which feature(s) can be done by the deadline so you don't over-commit yourself to the largest and most complex feature that the client is hoping to have and which you may not be able to complete by that date.

When providing your pricing for a client's project (assuming you're confident in your ability to complete it), then be sure to restate the scope of work you plan on delivering for them. Really put it in as much detail as you can.

Don't tell them HOW you'll be doing it (and giving away your secrets), but informing the client WHAT you'll be doing, that it will be done in a way to ensure their live site is safe and protected (performed on a staging environment), what your development process looks like, when you'll be able to deliver it, and then what your price will be.

An example development process might look something like this: Initial Consultation, Briefing and Concepts, Work Begins, Testing, Production, Handover. You'll of course want to break down your own dev. process to the client and be sure to go into additional detail of what each stage looks like, how many revisions are included, how it will be tested (including what browsers and devices it will be tested on), what the handover looks like and if it will include any documentation or training, etc...

Then ask the client if they have any questions they'd like answered before proceeding. There may be a concern or objection that the client has and if you leave it like "here's my price" and that's it, it can close out the conversation. By leaving it more open, you're inviting the client to ask you questions, which helps to keep the client engaged. It also shows their needs, desires, and goals are your top priority.

And if the cost is higher than they anticipated, then don't just say "Sorry then, I can't help you". Try to work with them to reduce the cost. I'll caution against lowering your price just because the client asks. This can lead to clients thinking your prices are all negotiable and that perhaps you were trying to overcharge them initially.

Instead, offer a reduced scope of work that might be more aligned with the budget they have allocated. Maybe if they have a list of 5 updates they'd like made, but their budget only allows for 3 of those updates, let them know which you can do for their budget. Or even better, ask which of the 5 updates are the most important and you can then re-adjust your pricing just for those items.

You might also consider offering alternate solutions that better align with their budget. For example, if the client is wanting a custom feature coded into their site, but their budget doesn't allow for it, then perhaps there's an existing plugin that gets them close to what they want.

Maybe it doesn't do everything 100% as they were originally asking for, but if it can get them 80% of the way there, and is more aligned with their budget, then consider asking the client to use this plugin. Then in your estimate, you can include the cost to install and properly configure this new plugin, possibly styling it to match the look of their site, and of course performing the work on a staging environment. This is all value-added work and much more than the client will be able to comfortably do themselves (i.e. install their own plugin).

Chapter Four

Charging More

(While Delivering More Value)

It sounds hard, but it's actually quite easy to charge more and just takes believing in yourself and knowing you're worth it.

To give you a quick example, people can go out and buy a knit shirt that does NOT have the Polo Ralph Lauren horse on it and the cost is around $10. But people choose to buy an official Polo shirt for $70 dollars because the perceived value is higher. People think because it's more expensive it's a nicer quality shirt and they are also buying the status of owning the Polo shirt.

Why are people willing to spend 7x more money for a Polo shirt? Is the quality 7x better?

No, it's really not. It might be slightly better, maybe slightly nicer buttons or slightly nicer stitching. But not 7x nicer.

Clients are paying for more than just code on a screen. They're paying to have their problem solved. They're paying to have a working solution that's been tested thoroughly. They're paying to not risk their live website crashing in the process of the update. They're paying to not look foolish to their boss if it doesn't work right. They're also paying for the above-average communication and experience you'll be providing.

Clients are paying for a lot of things when they hire you. You should be charging your worth to ensure a quality job from start to finish. This includes things like:

- charging to clone the website over to staging...

- charging to create a repo...

- charging to perform the actual work...

- charging to QA the work...

- charging to push the changes to live...

- charging for the back-forth communication you'll be having with the client...

- charging for the unexpected challenges that often arise (at least 30% of the total quote you have in mind) and which need to be resolved before the job is done...

- charging for aftercare (meaning if something doesn't work on the live environment but it works properly on staging...

All of these things cost money and true professionals charge for their time for all of this. You should be also. And if there is something that won't be included in your charge, ie the aftercare portion, then be sure to let the client know up-front in your proposal/scope of work that this is not included and will incur an additional charge if something should break on the live environment.

There's something called the Imposter Syndrome which can have an effect on even brilliant developers because they feel like others know more than they do.

Don't let this stop you or hold you back.

I know you. You're resourceful. You're intelligent. You'll figure out the solution one way or another. Yes, you may have to invest a bit more time than you originally expected, but think of this as a learning experience. You'll be upgrading your skillset and knowledge of WordPress and specific themes and plugins when you're working to figure out an issue that you come across. Have faith in yourself that you can do it and take a chance on yourself.

What's the worst thing that can happen?

So long as this isn't an urgent project, you'll simply realize you really aren't able to complete their request and you offer them a refund. All of the work was done on a staging environment and so their live website is still intact and unaltered. Or if you've finished part of the scope of work, say 5 out of their 10 requested items, then consider offering the client a partial refund to account for the tasks that weren't done. Apologize to the client and see if they'd like to keep the work that was done. If they decide they don't want it, then don't provide it to them and simply refund their money paid. If they do want to keep the work, then allow them to keep it and process the partial refund for them.

The best baseball players in the world, those in the hall of fame have a batting average of 300. This means that they strike out 7 out of 10 times they're up to bat. It's impossible to bat 1000 and get a run on base every time, so keep this in mind when you're looking into taking on a project. Know that you'll never satisfy and complete 100% of the projects you take on. This is life and you need to get over trying to be perfect. Just be confident knowing you're going to do your best (maybe you'll end up putting in a bit more work/time than you anticipated) and most projects you work on will likely result in a win.

If you don't know or aren't sure how to accomplish something, or you're not sure how long it will take, just take your best guess and try to include as much of a buffer as possible so in case it takes longer than expected, you're still covering most of your hours on the project.

If it's a complex project or there are several un-knowns in the work to be done, you might also consider using a more agile approach with the client.

Explain how agile development works, that you'll like to work based on time-sheets, and that you'd like to begin with 10 hour blocks (please use your own blocks here; they could be 5 hours or 20 hours as well). It may also be that you charge half-day or full-day blocks or even week-long sprints.

Let the client know what you plan to accomplish in this block of time, and you'll communicate status updates with the client at least 1x per week (more is better). Then after each block, you'll report on what work was done, what issues or challenges came up, and what you plan to work on for the next block.

I also recommend scheduling at least weekly check-in calls with the client so you can communicate the status updates with them live and answer any questions they might have. This helps to keep the trust level high and they know you're actually getting work done and not watching Netflix on their dollar. And of course the client will pay you for each block before you get started on it.

In my experience, it's always easier to get paid before you start working versus playing bill collector and trying to get paid after the work has been done.

I realize I'm using the assumption and calculation of trading time for money and it can be argued that value-based pricing is a better model to use versus fixed-cost or even agile where the client is paying for your actual time spent on the project.

I agree with you, value-based pricing is excellent and I highly recommend beginning to incorporate this into your pricing model and work-flow. This can be a bit more challenging though, especially for newer developers who maybe don't yet have the experience working with clients and charging higher rates.

If you know the client, what industry they're in, how much they can afford, how much revenue they generate, and how much new revenue they will generate after you implement your solution for them, then, by all means, use a value-based pricing approach.

In this case, you might consider thinking through how much money they will be able to earn after you implement this new solution for them. If you calculate that this will increase their revenue by $20,000 per year, then charging 10% – 20% should make sense to them and be affordable enough for them to proceed with you. They will see a return on their investment (ROI) within 1-2 months and each month after will be all profit for them.

But if you don't know the answers to the questions above, then using an hourly rate-based pricing model (or agile for complex projects) may be simpler. You can determine the hourly rate you wish to earn (I would suggest at least $100 per hour), and multiply the amount of time you feel the project will take, the complexity of the project, the urgency, and add a 30% buffer to the top (for the unexpected).

When thinking through the scope of work and how long you believe it will take you to complete it, make sure to include the time needed for tasks such as:

- cloning the site to staging...

- setting up the repo...

- performing the actual work...

- QA'ing the work...

- deploying it to live...

- communicating with the client...

- potential aftercare, etc...

As an aside, some developers in the Top 2% actually _exclude_ the pushing the staging back to live. They instead turn this into a separate task as there can be unforeseen complications and too many unknowns when pushing the staging over to the live environment. I'm not saying you need to charge for this separately, but do take it into consideration.

Also take into account the urgency of the project, meaning if it's a really urgent request, then consider charging a premium for this. Consider the complexity of the request and if it's a very complex task, then again charge a premium and add more to your hourly rate.

Don't forget about adding a buffer of around 30% to whatever the total amount of time you think it will take. Meaning if you think it will take you 10 hours to complete, then charge for 13 hours.

To put this into an actual scenario, imagine you're given a request that you feel will take 10 hours to complete and your normal hourly rate is $100 per hour. This is a fairly complex request and there are some unknown variables. So you might consider charging $130 per hour due to this complexity.

The client has made it clear this is an urgent request and wants you to work over the weekend to have it ready by Monday. So now instead of $130 per hour, you're using a rate of $160 per hour.

Since you're using the estimate of 10 hours, you'll multiply the 10 hours x $160 and end up with $1,600. Then add your 30% buffer to the top and you'll arrive at $2,080.

The client will not care about the difference of a few hundred dollars and it won't be felt at all by them. And if you're working for a client who is an employee at an agency or company, it's not even their money. In this case, they care more about having the job done right, no risk to their live website, and knowing they can give you the request and it'll be done and they won't risk looking foolish in front of their boss. **This is peace of mind for the client** and they will pay your premium for this.

As a quick disclaimer, use pricing that you feel is appropriate for your skill level. In the above example, I'm assuming you're a senior developer in which case you should be charging what you're worth. But use your own rates.

If you're a junior developer and don't quite have the experience of a senior level developer, then don't pretend to be a senior developer and charge senior developer rates.

I'm not encouraging you to rip off clients or over-charge them. I'm wanting you to use your best judgment on what you feel is a fair rate for you. Don't under-charge for your services, but don't over-charge either.

I'm not going to keep saying this throughout the remaining chapters, but always act in a responsible and ethical manner. Still, consider using the calculation above, but perhaps adjusting down your hourly rate from $100 to maybe $60 until you have the skill level and experience to charge more.

Chapter Five

How To Get Better At Pricing Projects

Assuming you're charging adequate rates, rates you know you're worth, which should hopefully be in the $100+ per hour range, how do you still protect yourself with your pricing to make sure you're anticipating enough time to complete the project without under-estimating your time and amount you're getting paid?

This can be a bit challenging, and while much of it is directly related to the scope of work being requested, it's still possible to under-estimate the amount of time a project can take.

I was recently speaking with a developer friend who was working on a project to optimize the performance of a client's site.

The developer provided the client with an estimate and included the scope of work that was to be completed in exchange for the price. The developer was to clone the site to staging, perform various speed optimization tasks, including the installation and configuration of WP Rocket, optimize all images, minify all JS/CSS, install and configure a CDN, and various other implementations to get the client's site loading faster.

After several days, the project was complete. At least that's what the developer thought.

The client was informed that the work was done and to please review and send the other 50% of their payment for the work that was done, at which point the developer will migrate all of the changes to the live site.

Upon the client's review, they began discovering a number of errors and differences comparing the staging site to the live site.

The developer was a bit confused and not being a frontend developer, was having difficulty seeing any of the differences and so they asked for the client to please show specifically where the issues were.

This annoyed the client right away. They felt like this wasn't their responsibility as they weren't expecting to have to do any work, and is why they hired a professional.

The client also felt that thet paid more than what was being offered on sites like UpWork where they had received bids of $500, but they wanted to go to someone who charged higher rates to get a more professional service and paid $1500. So the client felt like this QA work should be done by the developer since it was so much more expensive.

I ended up helping my developer friend by bringing both sites side-by-side on my screen and took many screenshots with arrows showing the differences between the two sites. Things like fonts being different, font weights, some images not loading properly or only loading after a refresh... columns appearing different, checkmarks in a list becoming normal bullet points, image galleries not loading... I personally came up with 6-8 things that were appearing different on the staging site compared to the live site.

The developer worked on it a couple more days, then informed the client the work was done and to please review and confirm everything was looking good now. The client came back with more differences and discovered more issues, this time on the mobile version of the site.

By this time, the client had lost confidence in the developer and felt like this person really didn't know what they were doing and was saying they want a refund of the 50% that they had already paid so that they could try their luck over on UpWork.

In speaking with the developer about this situation, they couldn't understand why the client was getting so upset and wanting to cancel the project.

The dev felt this was a normal part of the QA process, and that the client never requested or paid for QA to be done and so this responsibility lies with the client and not the developer. The client's role in the project is to perform the QA, let the developer know what the issues are, and he'd resolve them.

But you see, the client didn't know their role was to perform QA. They felt like this was the responsibility of the developer, especially since they were paying a higher price.

So what can the developer do moving forward to help prevent this from happening in the future?

Communication is the key.

More clear communication and asking more questions pre-hire...

For example, I've seen where clients expect the developer to provide all paid stock images for a new site-build. Of course, the developer assumed the client would be providing the images. As a result it was never discussed and became an issue halfway into the project.

One thing to bring attention to involves asking the client up-front, who will be handling things like QA or paid stock images?

Chances are the client is under the impression that you're the professional and you should be handling these things. Many developers are under the impression that if the client doesn't ask about including specific parts of the dev process, that must mean that the client will be handling it.

As a result, nobody is expecting to perform those tasks and therefore it's not done. This results in the client feeling like they're working with a sloppy developer who doesn't even check their work or is too cheap to buy a handful of images.

So 1 main takeaway here is to ask these types of questions pre-hire and BEFORE giving the client your price to complete their project request.

I'll suggest breaking the project into granular pieces, and before any pricing is given, asking the client who will be completing things like QA and explaining what that means. The client may say *'No, you do that'*. In which case, you'll want to include additional hours and charges into the total price.

Then if the client receives the price and says that's higher than they anticipated, then you can offer to remove things like QA, again explaining that this role will be left to the client, and you can reduce the price accordingly.

Or offer to reduce the scope of work another way, such as reducing the number of tasks that will be done, or finding other solutions to accomplish the same or similar results.

For example, if the client wants a custom theme created and to implement their Photoshop design, but doesn't have the budget for a custom theme, then perhaps offer a premium theme that incorporates the client's design.

But make sure to ask these important questions up front as they can have a direct impact on the amount of time you invest and the amount of money you charge.

Another takeaway is to learn from each and every project.

In the previous example, the developer should ideally document this project, what the request was and what was learned during the course of working on the project. This will allow them to more accurately price out a future similar project.

If the developer doesn't document these details, it's possible they'll get another similar project request in the future. And it's possible they'll remember enough of these details to price it fairly accurately. But this isn't how a developer in *The Top 2%*, a WP Dev Hero, does things.

We don't leave these things to chance. This is directly related to the amount of money you earn and should be treated with the utmost care and respect.

With these details properly documented, you'll be able to price your projects much more accurately, more easily recall the small details that can make a big difference (like who handles the QA), and as a result, more accurately price your projects.

Then with these documented details, you'll also be able to mine your past client data to see who has a theme or plugins that have recently received an update and could use your skill and expertise to safely update the client's site... but we'll talk more about this in Chapter 10 on Documenting Client's Projects and what you're able to do with this data once you have it.

Chapter Six

How To Charge To Troubleshoot A Website Issue

This is a pretty common challenge that I hear from WordPress developers. When a client comes to them with an issue, and the cause or solution isn't known, it can be hard to tell the client a price.

Charge too much and you'll scare the client away. Charge too little and you could be on the hook for working for 10 hours when you only charged the client for 2, so your earnings per hour go down the toilet.

So what's the best way to approach a debugging or troubleshooting task with a client?

I've spoken with a lot of WP devs about this and this seems to be one of the best ways we've found to handle these...

Depending on the issue, many WP Dev Heroes will request an initial troubleshooting phase of 3 hours so they can look into what's needed to be done to solve the issue.

Or if the issue appears to be more complex, for example, troubleshooting issues with a Multisite, then it may be more appropriate to start with a half day (4 hours) or full day (8 hours) discovery phase to even better protect your time.

Let the client know that sometimes the issue is solved in this initial block of hours and that's always your goal going into it. If it is solved in the initial 3 hours, that's great! But make sure to let the client know up-front that it's not a guarantee to have it solved and it may take that long to find the issue and once the exact issue is known, then it can be priced to actually fix the issue.

To help the client feel even better about this, you can also let the client know if you find and fix the issue in let's say 1 hour, then you will be happy to refund the unused time back to them. Then the client will feel even more comfortable proceeding.

Please make sure they understand that you'll be doing an initial discovery and you're going to be bug hunting in that time and there's no guarantee you'll find the issue and solve it within the 3 hours.

I can't stress enough how **communication is key.** Be honest and open and ask them to confirm and agree that they understand and would like to proceed with this option. Then you'll ask your client to pay for the 3 hours (or whichever amount you decide to begin with) for you to get started.

It's also a great idea to let the client know what they can expect after the 3-hour session is up. For example, you should provide a summary of what areas were checked, what was tested, and what your findings are.

Hopefully, in these 3 hours, you'll be able to narrow down what the issue is and then inform the client of your results (the summary).

In the summary, you should include your idea of what the specific bug is, where it is, what you will need to do to resolve the bug and fix it, and a cost for doing this.

Then the client will be able to decide if the cost is worth it to solve this bug, or if it's not too critical, then perhaps leave it as-is. But at least the client knows the details and cost involved and can make an informed decision.

And since you'll have everything in writing and in your agreement from the beginning, there shouldn't be any issues or complaints about the money already invested. The client knew what they were "signing up for" and made the decision and agreement to continue with this method and paid your fee knowing what they will get at the end of the 3 hours (which may not be a full resolution of the issue).

Chapter Seven

How To Deliver Your Price To The Client

I t really doesn't matter what you're selling. It could be a pen, a car, a computer, or development services, people rarely buy from you if all they have to go on is the price.

How much is this pen?

It's $225.

No thanks, I can buy a BIC pen for 50 cents, bye.

How much is this car?

It's $100,000.

No thanks, I can buy a Kia Sorento for $10,000, bye.

How much is this computer?

It's $2,500.

No thanks, I can buy a Chromebook for $250, bye.

How much does it cost to resolve this SSL issue with my site's Vimeo player?

It's $235.

No thanks, too expensive, bye...

It sounds kind of silly while I type this, but I've seen WordPress developers do this when a client asks for a price to resolve their issue or perform a task for them.

I've seen some brilliant WP developers engage with a client, ask some really great questions, build up the rapport, only to have the conversation completely die when they provide the price to the client and so often it's just that, the price. Take it or leave it.

So how is it that Monte Blanc pens sell every day for $225, all the way up to $1,650? After all, it's just a pen isn't it? Or is it?

Or how about the $100,000 Mercedes that people buy every day when a $10,000 Kia can get them from point A to point B just the same?

Or a $2,500 Apple MacBook Pro when they could buy a $250 Chromebook?

People aren't just buying a pen, or a car or a computer, the same way they aren't just buying development work. There's actually quite a bit more they're buying whether they realize it consciously or not.

What else could you be selling then if it's not just development services?

How about peace of mind knowing that the work will be carried out on a staging environment so their company website won't risk going down?

How much do you think that safety and security are worth to someone, especially someone who's an employee?

It's not the client's credit card that's being charged for the work to be done and their paycheck won't be impacted one bit if the solution costs $200 or $500. But if the company website crashes after they contracted the work out to you, do you think the client will be landing in hot water with their boss? You bet they will!

So there is a way to properly frame the work that is to be carried out for the client, in a way that really shows your value? A way that can help the client justify the cost to their superior?

(This doesn't only apply to a company website. It could be a spouse or significant other's blog that they're helping to maintain and if they hire the wrong developer and the blog crashes, who do you think will be sleeping on the couch?)

I noticed some of *The Top 2%* of developers are doing a phenomenal job of engaging with clients, asking beautiful questions, really taking their time with the client to build the rapport, strengthen the client's trust in them, then it comes time for the price...

This is where the conversation can potentially take a COMPLETELY different turn and the developer says something along the lines of...

"I am ready to help you with this and the total cost is $XXX..."

or *"The total cost will be $XXX...Looking forward to assisting you with this."*

And that's it.

That's often where the conversation dies.

Often times, the client is receiving a price that is higher than they anticipated it would be. After all, they aren't developers themselves, they don't know how much something will cost.

Or more accurately stated, how much it will cost when doing things the right way, the quality way...

So please take another moment to help the client feel comfortable proceeding with you.

Consider asking the client if they have any questions that they would like answered...

Or explaining to them some of the information about the work involved to complete their request so they can better justify the cost and why it's so much.

For example, someone who I consider to be a WP Dev Hero really nailed it with their message to the client that was sent along with the cost to complete their request:

Hi John,

Please allow me to explain a bit about the process and what's included in my price of $1000.

I will start by taking full measurements of the current site and I'll be creating matching headers and matching footers.

Once the header and footer match the current style I will proceed to set up and style the sidebar to match the current website.

After the sidebar is a match, I will make sure the single post, archive and content templates are cloned.

All work will be done on a staging environment so that your live website isn't impacted at all and your users will not experience any downtime while the work is progressing. After you've had a chance to review everything and you give me the green-light, only then will I push the changes from the staging website to your live website.

All of your content will remain the same and at the end of the process, you will have a beautiful and matching lightweight Genesis theme that matches your live site.

Let me know if you have any additional questions, and I'll be happy to answer them for you.

Thanks so much,
Chris

Clients need to sometimes justify the cost to themselves (or maybe even their business partner, boss, spouse, or significant other) and also feel good about proceeding with you.

Help them feel good and confident knowing you're their right choice!

Here's another great real-world example showing the flip-side of when a project can reach an untimely demise.

A bit of context; this is an actual project where a developer takes time to engage with a repeat client over Skype, asks great questions, then provides a price. Let's see what happens...

Client's initial message:

Hi Sally, I'm displaying all my work using Vimeo player, and none of the videos on my website will currently load due to an SSL conflict. If I disable the secure URL, they will play, but this is less than ideal. I spoke to a representative at SiteGround and they said there was a conflict in SSL between Vimeo and my website. I'm not really sure how to fix it and I'm hoping you can do it fairly quickly. If you need any more information let me know.

Developer Reply:

Hi Bill,

I would love to help with this and I have a few questions:

Do you use a plugin to show the video in a grid or is it part of your theme?

What's your timeframe on this?

After we clarify everything I will be happy to send you a quote and start with your task asap.

Thank you in advance!
Sally

Client:

Hi Sally,

Thanks for getting back to me,

1) I assume it's part of the theme I purchased from ThemeForest. Not sure if that uses a particular plugin.

2) I am hoping to start applying for jobs in the near future and having my website work properly would be ideal. At this stage ASAP is fine.

It was working a couple of months back, it seems to have developed recently when I renewed my website with SiteGround.

Thanks again.

Developer:

Thanks, Bill. Do you use the latest version of your theme?

Client:

Im using Version: 2.06

Developer:

It looks like your theme is Red: Folio

Just looking into it further now...

It looks like the theme is not supported by the theme author anymore.

Not to worry though, I can fix it and the cost will be $235.

Client:

Thanks, Sally, but that's more than I was expecting.

Developer:

No problem, I understand

The request has just died.

The client is left without a solution and the developer has wasted time looking into it.

What should have been done here is to provide value WITH the price. You really need to help the client understand what is needed to be done so then the client can better justify the cost needed to resolve the issue...

An example of a reply **after informing** the client of
the price would be to state something along the lines
of:

Developer:

> *Unfortunately, it looks like this won't be
> a quick and simple fix as you might have
> been hoping for.*
>
> *It's looking like this is a misconfiguration
> of the web server (or load balancer), and
> that can be a bit trickier to sort through. I'll
> need to look through your Nginx/Apache
> config files to see how 443 is being handled.*
>
> *I'll also be checking if there are any odd set-
> tings pertaining to the ports or any strange
> redirection commands, particularly check-
> ing files in sites-available. If you are on
> a shared hosting plan with SiteGround, I
> may need to talk to their support team be-
> cause they control server configuration and
> so I may need to get their assistance with*

making the necessary updates.

It could also be that your theme is force loading Vimeo videos with only HTTP - it could be hardcoded in the shortcode - but I cannot check this through the editor in WordPress and will need to dig through the theme's coding to determine this.

If this theme was still being supported by the original developer/company, you may have been able to ask their support team for assistance, but since it's no longer supported, this likely won't be an option.

I'm happy to help you with this and can have it completed within 1 day. I'll also be working on a staging environment to make sure your live website is safe throughout the process. Did you have any questions for me before getting started?

I know what some of you might be thinking - *this is a lot of work!* But this actually only took me 3 minutes to Google and find this information, and another 3 minutes to type up.

It's not giving away the solution because if the client has this issue, they don't have the technical know-how to fix it themselves, otherwise, they wouldn't be talking with you and asking for your help in the first place.

And you've already invested 15 minutes into the conversation with the client. So why not spend another 6 to greatly increase your chance of getting hired?

When you're hired, then it's a win! If you stop with "*Here's my price.*" then you likely won't get hired and you'll have wasted all your time on it anyway.

Providing this little bit of additional value with your price WILL have an impact on your number of paid projects and you'll have another happy client after it's done who will trust you, like you, and want to work with you again... all because you took time to explain things to them.

By taking a few extra minutes to explain what needs to be done, the client understands this isn't just 2-clicks and it's solved. It's not like a checkbox that needs to be clicked that they're just not seeing. With that kind of perception, it's much easier to think that this should be simple and this person is just over-charging me.

So take some extra time to explain it in some detail and the client can then justify the cost involved, like *'Wow, that IS a lot of work... I had no idea! This does seem like a fair price and I'll make the investment to have this work done, and done properly.'*

Hopefully you can see and feel the difference and understand how to provide more value when delivering your price to the client.

Chapter Eight

How To Approach And Land Larger Projects

I know many developers who only focus on larger clients with larger projects and budgets. While this is certainly possible to do, it does take a more skillful and professional approach. There's also greater risk involved working with a new client, whose personality you don't yet know, with more money on the line, and with a potential for a longer waiting period before getting paid in full.

I also know developers who will work with clients on several smaller size projects, and then after having great experiences working together, the client will need a new site design or other larger project and who do you think they'll reach out to? Their trusted developer who has consistently delivered great results for them in the past.

So 1 strategy that works very well, is to find clients with smaller size projects, between $100-500.

Get to learn the client; are they abusive or always professional when engaging with you?

If the client is abusive and demanding on smaller projects, is this someone you'd like to work with on larger projects where there's more money at stake and more risk involved? If so, you'd better charge accordingly.

Does the client need a lot of handholding, or are they trusting of you and quick to understand what you're telling them?

If they need extra hand-holding and explaining of things, make sure to include that additional markup into your price you provide them. You may be needing to have lots of phone calls and take extra time to explain things in very detailed ways, so again charge accordingly.

Is the client responsive to your questions and requests? Or do they disappear for days and weeks at a time?

If a client takes days or even weeks to respond, you'll want to consider charging more and breaking the project down into smaller milestones so that the client will continue funding the project as progress is being made. If they disappear, it's annoying and frustrating, but at least you can wait for them to come back and take on additional projects in the meantime.

Does the client always try to scope creep on you, or do they understand new requests all cost additional money?

If you have a client who consistently scope creeps on you when it's a smaller project, how much scope creep might be involved in a project 10x the size?

Assuming you do decide to work on larger projects, there are some additional ways to protect yourself.

The first is like we just mentioned, know your client so you can provide an accurate price for the work involved. Since you'll have previous experience working with this person, you may wish to include an additional buffer to account for the added calls or explaining you might need to do, or for delays in waiting for replies, or for the scope creep that will likely be coming.

The other option to consider, is when going after larger projects, to make sure you charge for any type of consulting or discovery phase that might be needed before the project kicks off.

I'd like to take a moment to share a recent conversation I had with a freelance WordPress developer based in Argentina.

He's a nice developer, very smart, and he enjoys creating custom plugins for clients.

On his website however, he portrays himself more as a generalist, a jack-of-all trades, and only briefly touches on custom plugins.

He didn't know what the point of consultations are, how they worked, or why he should consider using them in his sales process.

I explained he needs to begin by updating his website to be centered around custom plugin development. Before he starts going after this niche, he needs to take some time to really update his website to reflect his speciality.

He should also be updating his social media profiles, his business cards, and anywhere else he has his name out there. He needs to OWN the custom plug-in development space and become THE Expert. Remember, the money is in the specialization... just like doctors who specialize in a particular field earn an average of 2x more than a general practitioner.

Then when he's talking to potential clients, he should explain that based on the size and complexity of the project, that the first step is to begin with a consultation for around $50. The idea is to not try and get rich from the consultation, but to protect your time and to earn a small bit of money for taking time with the potential client. This also changes the relationship from a freebie-seeker to a paying client and there's important psychology at play here.

Go into what will be discussed on a consultation call, how long the call will last, and what the value is that will be received at the end (i.e. deliverable).

An example might include; up to one hour on the phone to discuss the desired outcomes of the client's project in detail... that you'll plan to do a bit of research and prepare a detailed agenda for the call (so you know what you'll be talking about on the call and you can prepare questions you'll need to know in order to build out the custom plugin... and that the deliverable will include a summary of your discussion together and what the next steps will be...

Then on the consultation call:

- ask questions about the client's business and their goals...

- what they want to achieve with the custom plugin, etc...

- explain how a custom plugin will be able to get them to their goal...

- summarize and review what the development process looks like...

Your development process for example may include beginning with a Discovery phase that includes X, Y, Z...

These are the steps you will be taking the client through. For example; a phone call, investigation, scope of work doc, etc.. basically, telling the client these are the deliverables you will receive at the end of the discovery phase for $XXX.

I'll suggest charging in the range of $300-1,000 for the discovery phase and work to over-deliver on the value that is received. Meaning don't charge $300 and deliver $150 worth of value. Put more time and attention into it, go into good detail, present a nicely formatted scope of work doc in a .pdf format with your brand's colors, fonts, etc.

Then on the backend of the discovery and the delivery of the discovery (scope of work doc), schedule a followup call with the client to walk them through the full game plan, milestones, cost breakdowns, delivery schedule, etc... everything that is included in your scope of work doc.

The beginning consultation stage serves 3 important purposes.

1.) It's meant as a screening method to see if the client is serious. Are they willing to pay the $50? If they won't pay the $50, chances are very high they won't pay the $2k-10k+ that you'll be charging for the custom plugin.

As mentioned earlier, the $50 covers a bit of your time for the call. It can be thought of as an investment into the larger project that will be coming on the backend of the call where you will more than make up for the initial time invested.

2.) The consultation is protecting your time, so you don't waste too much time trying to scope it out, only to discover the client is expecting a $5k plugin for $300. Better to find this out early before you've invested too much time into it.

3.) The consultation is a great way to step the client up to the larger project amount. Really, the progression should go; $50 Consultation —> $300-1,000 Discovery Phase —> the full project broken down into milestones with the first being $1,000+.

This "Stepping-Up" method is a much lower risk to both you and the client. You get to learn more about the client; are they a nice person, do you enjoy working with them, are they professional, do they respond back to you in a timely manner, do they ask 100 questions on everything (i.e. how much handholding is there), etc...

So use the consultation and discovery phase to learn about the client and see if it's someone you'd like to be married to for the next 2 months or more. If you get a bad feeling right at the beginning, trust your gut and fire the client or don't continue on with the next phase. It's not worth the stress or anxiety to work with a toxic client when there are other better clients out there.

In contrast, by going straight in for the sale and to ask a client who doesn't know you, has never spoken with you, for $5,000, it's a really big ask.

Instead, when you Step-Up the client from a simple free request, to a $50 consultation, then it's only $50 at risk and the client is much more comfortable with that. It's very low risk.

Then on the $50 consultation call, you're able to talk with the client, they can hear your voice, they can see your face (I always recommend a video call when possible), they can hear the great questions you're asking and you displaying your knowledge and enthusiasm about what's needed. Then they're beginning to feel comfortable with you. The rapport is building .They've spent the $50 and haven't been let down and left to feel foolish and it feels like a good investment both of money and time.

Then on the $50 call, you explain the next step in the development process is to begin with a discovery phase. Here again, you're stepping the client up into a slightly larger ask; $500 let's say. Still not a huge amount, but certainly larger than the initial $50.

When you show your professionalism and over-deliver on the $500 discovery, and deliver a nicely formatted and nicely presented scope of work doc, they will feel even more comfortable with you. They've invested $500 and didn't get ripped off, and they're again feeling good with their investment, receiving value, you're building even more rapport, establishing even more trust with the client. You're now showing them the path forward to actually getting the custom plugin they need developed and launched for their site.

The last step is to explain on the discovery delivery call, what you've delivered, walk them through each page of the scope doc, and explain what the next step in the process is (i.e. beginning with the wire-framing for $1,000, or starting with the design, etc...).

Again the client will have had 2 previous transactions with you, both successful, both were delivered as expected. So this next phase of $1,000, while it's larger, is the natural progression of the relationship and project and chances are much higher of the client proceeding with you having had those 2 earlier successful transactions.

Versus going straight for the $5,000 ask right away on the first interaction. It's important to note also that the client is becoming more invested with you because if they were to make a switch to a new developer at this stage, they will be out both time and money.

Like I said, someone who won't invest the original $50 for the consultation, is very unlikely to give you $5,000 when the time comes. It's a very large ask and a challenging sale to make. Possible, but not as likely to happen and you really need to have positioned yourself so incredibly well that your reputation precedes you.

An additional strategy to help sell the idea (and cost) of a consultation or discovery phase to the client, is to offer to provide a credit (discount) of an equal amount off the total project cost. So if the client decides to proceed to work with you on the actual project, they'll have not lost (or spent) any money.

On larger projects, you may also wish to make the scope of work document into an actual contractual agreement holding both parties accountable for the work and deadlines. This can help to protect you in case of any disputes that turn into lawsuits. You'll want to contact an attorney in your country or town to help you with creating the template for this document so that it can stand up in court if needed.

I'll also suggest including verbiage into the contract (scope of work) that holds the client accountable for any delays in communicating or delivering assets to you and which may result in a missed deadline.

You'll want to factor this into your deadlines as well; something along the lines of giving the client 48 hours to respond to all communication requests otherwise you, the developer, will not be held accountable for the missed deadline(s).

I've even seen some professional developers have a clause in the contract that the developer reserves the right to charge the client for delays in the project. Not that you will always be charging the client and it's good to not be a jerk about it, but just so that it's in there and that you reserve this right in case things get ugly.

One method a professional developer that I know uses to reduce scope creep on larger projects is to make a list of all additional out of scope requests and documents each one with a price next to it.

After the list starts getting too long, the developer shares the list with the client and informs them that any new requests after this last one and they'll need to charge the client for all of the out of scope items on the list.

When the client sees the big list and all the additional money they would have to pay, they think very carefully about if the new request is really worth it. This appears to be working well for the developer and has reduced his scope creep quite a bit.

Speaking of reducing scope creep, we'll dive even deeper into this in the next chapter as it's a fairly common issue many developers face.

If you decide to go straight for the larger sales up-front, I highly recommend that you position yourself as the expert and as a celebrity. When dealing with larger sales, and as you move up the income ladder, it's been said that *'You get paid more for <u>Who you are</u>, than for <u>What</u> you do.'*

You still need to be great at what you do, there's no denying or getting around that. But there are ways to manufacture celebrity status and authority, which will make it much easier to command higher prices and land larger projects. We'll cover this in more detail in Chapter 15: Manufacturing Celebrity.

Chapter Nine

How To Reduce And Even Prevent Scope Creep

This is a problem that has plagued developers forever. While some clients don't even realize they are engaging in scope creep, the additional requests being made by the client can add up to additional time invested into the project and can lead to lost revenue and never-ending projects.

It can be tricky if you allow a few additional requests in, as it may open the door allowing the client to take advantage of your goodwill and accommodating nature to continue making the requests.

So how do you reduce or even prevent scope creep?

It starts with having a solid Scope of Work (SOW) or proposal that's agreed to up front.

Carefully explaining the details of what the project scope will include and informing the client that any additional requests outside of this will cost additional money.

You'll want to be as specific as possible in this stage to clearly articulate things like:

- How many pages will be included and what constitutes a page, i.e. number of words?

- Will a contact form be included? How many fields is the contact form? Is there going to be conditional logic involved?

- How many products will be included? Are there variable products? How many options for each product?

Scope creep most often occurs when a project has not been given enough thought beforehand and vague requests by the client are agreed to and priced out.

While it can be tempting to rush into a price with a client to land the project, it's always better to carefully consider the client's requests and ask additional clarifying questions about the work that's needing doing.

It's important that you clearly explain the Scope of Work to the client to make sure they're understanding of everything and there's no confusion. The time to ask questions is before the money exchanges hands and work begins—not after.

You'll want to explain your development process to the client, the steps involved, and what your requirements are/will be of the client.

What is the preferred method of communication while working with the client? Will you set up a Project Management tool like Trello, Basecamp, Asana, or Slack channel? If the client isn't responding back, do you have an alternate email address or phone number for the client so that you can call them if needed?

If you need the client to be available, state in your proposal that you will be responding to all of the client's inquiries and questions within X amount of time (1 business day is a good benchmark) and that you require the client to do the same. Or you could give the client 2 business days to respond to your requests and questions, otherwise, the deadline is at risk of being missed. So make sure to account for this in your delivery schedule.

Also clearly state in the proposal that if the client does not respond within the 2 business days timeframe, that not only can the deadline be impacted, but that you reserve the right to charge the client for these delays. Hopefully, it won't ever come to that, but if things take a turn for the worse, it's great to have this in writing and the client's agreement/signature on it.

Identify the milestones of the project with a delivery schedule (deadlines) included.

This will help to hold both parties accountable, not just you, the developer.

Consider what order the project needs to be completed in and when items are due from both parties.

Again, communication is key.

This is so important not just in working as a freelance developer, but with life in general. Communication really is key.

While keeping things in writing is ideal (so that there's a paper trail and things are clear and in black/white), sometimes the need will arise to hop on a call with the client.

In this situation, I always recommend developers to record phone conversations regardless of where they take place; Skype, Google Meet, WhatsApp, Facebook Messenger, Telephone... it really doesn't matter, the call should be recorded. Thankfully, there are apps for just about every modality the call could be made that allows you to record calls, or record your screen that includes audio. Or you can ask the client to hop on an UberConference call (it's free) and at the end, the recording will be provided to them.

> **Important: Make the client aware that you will be recording the call before you click record!!**

In most countries, it's illegal to record a conversation without the other parties' consent. So always ask for permission, and at the end of the call, let the client know you will be happy to send them a copy of the conversation.

This helps to prevent confusion later about the details of what was discussed.

Whether you record the conversation or not, AL-WAYS follow up with a quick message to the client discussing the details of what was discussed on the call. You might consider labeling this follow-up message "Minutes of Our Meeting [Date]". Keeping your projects organized is a must so that you can have all of your notes and scope requests in one place that's easy to find and access. This might be using Evernote or your project management tool that you use.

Then ask the client to please reply back to confirm your understanding of those details. This again protects you from a future dispute with a client who thinks something should be included in the Scope of Work because you discussed it on a call, and you don't recall that conversation ever coming up.

Get it in writing.

Yes, it takes an extra 5 minutes to type up a quick call summary, but it can literally save you hours and hours of additional out of scope work or possible legal troubles if the client decides to push back on scope creep saying they'll sue you if you don't work on these additional requests. By having this typed-up summary, it prevents you from having to re-listen to the entire previous meeting.

I recently heard from a successful freelance Word-Press developer who shared their strategy for addressing scope creep and I want to share it with you here...

When the client begins making out of scope requests, regardless of the size of the request, the developer acknowledges the client's request, lets them know that's a great idea and that they can help them with this.

Then the developer says, *'Let's finish up our current SOW and then at the end of the project, we'll review this request together.'*

Then he logs that request in a file so it won't be forgotten.

As you know, it's very likely that a client won't just have a single great idea or out of scope request, but there might be 5 really great ideas of what they'd like done that's additional.

Each time the request is made, they acknowledge the request, let them know they can help with it, and say let's review this together at the end of the project.

Then when you arrive at the end of the project, check to see how much time you have remaining in your budget. It's possible that you might finish up the project a bit early and you have time to help with 1 or 2 of their smaller requests.

It's important to let the client know that you finished a little bit early, you have X amount of time remaining, and so you'll be happy to help complete Tasks A and B for free. These might be smaller requests and you can fit them into the remaining budget.

But, for the other requests C, D, E, that these are a bit larger in scope and will require additional time invested to get these implemented.

Politely and professionally remind the client of the original scope of work that was agreed to and which the client paid, and that these requests are not a part of this main scope of work that was paid for.

Communicate with the client, determine the scope of the new requests, make sure you understand precisely what's needed to be done, and then provide the client with a new price to complete these new requests. And make sure to price it out using the method discussed in Chapter 4.

Clients are looking for a solution to their problem. So help them find this solution and give them a path forward.

Let the client know after scoping out the additional requests, that it'll cost $XXX and you can have it ready by Y date. Then ask if the client would like to proceed with this.

If the client pushes back at all, simply apologize and let them know unfortunately you aren't able to work further on these requests without additional payment. That you have other projects in your pipeline from paying clients and you need to be careful with your time.

IF looking back over the scope, you realize perhaps there is some vagueness and it's possible you didn't ask enough questions up front to better understand the client's requests, then consider offering the client a discount on the additional work. Basically, acknowledge your part in this confusion and offer to possibly meet them in the middle. If you were going to charge an additional $500, then perhaps only charge them

$250 or $300 since it's possible you may have not done the best job in scoping out the project.

Be honorable and own your mistakes and the client will surely appreciate your willingness to help and will likely proceed with paying the additional cost.

Here's an awesome strategy shared from a freelance WordPress developer who was working inside a WP VIP agency...

He stated that when he was working in the VIP agency, every single item in the SOW had a **User Story** attached to it. If you're not familiar with User Stories please take a moment to Google and learn about them.

Mike Cohn, of Mountain Goat software, has a terrific blog post titled 'User Stories' that I highly recommend reading. Basically, a User Story looks like this:

As a < type of user >, I want < some goal >, so that < some reason >.

To put it into an actual scenario:

As an admin, I want to backup my website, so that I can easily restore if my site crashes.

User Stories are a beautiful way of detailing the functionality being requested by the client and my friend said this virtually eliminated all scope creep from their VIP agency.

If a client makes an additional request, it can sometimes be challenging to push back on it when it's just a line item requirement in the scope of work.

I've seen where clients try to argue why its *"common sense"* that the user should be able to do this or click that, or access this certain area of the site.

Clients may not be technical and don't understand their simple *"common sense"* requests mean an additional 20 hours of development to complete.

When incorporating User Stories into your SOW, it makes it much easier to push back on a client in easy to understand terms.

How does this new request fit into the User Story we agreed to before the project began?

If it doesn't, then you have them and it's much easier to push back on the additional work being requested. Especially when you've already protected yourself earlier in the engagement stating in your proposal that all requests outside of this will be considered additional work and charged accordingly.

Remember to remain calm, and always professional.

Provide a new price for the additional work and allow the client to decide if it's worth it or not to include in this project.

They might say, *"Actually, since that's more than we can afford right now, let's leave this out for now and we might address it later on down the road."* Or they'll say, *"Yes, this is something that we really need and I didn't think of it earlier, so yes please proceed and I'll pay the additional amount."*

Either way, you need to let the client decide for themselves. And if you've included enough markup (buffer) into your original quote that was paid, then it's possible there will be time leftover at the end of the project to include an additional request, but you'll need to wait until the end of the project to see how much time (and budget) is remaining in the original amount paid and agreed to.

At the end of the day, the client has an issue or problem that they need you to resolve. So be ready to offer them a solution. It doesn't (and shouldn't) be a free solution and come at the expense of you and your time, but you should offer them a solution and see if they're willing to pay for it.

As a quick caveat, you might perhaps take into consideration the individual client, how much you enjoy working with them, how much they have paid you, and the size of the new out of scope request.

I was recently speaking with a developer who was working with a client who has been very nice throughout the entire project. The client's professional, paying whatever was asked and who had invested over $25,000 into a project spread out over 4 milestones in a matter of a few months.

When the client made a smaller request that took the developer about 20 minutes to implement (adding an additional field to a CSV export), the developer didn't push back at all and happily offered to help with it. The client soon after paid an additional $5,700 for further development.

Had the developer pushed back and requested the client to pay $30-50 for this request, the client would have very likely paid it, but what might that have done to the relationship and on-going future work?

There's a time and a place to push back on out of scope requests and use your best judgment.

While these strategies work great for **New Requests**, what about when a client says there's a Bug in the work you've done and they ask you to fix it?

This can turn into a real challenge if you're not ready for it. If you don't look into the bug, then the client feels you've ripped them off and delivered poor quality code and aren't standing behind your work. Things can turn ugly quick.

If you do fix the bug, and it wasn't a result of your work, then you're losing money by working on it for free.

Allow me to share a quick real-world example of a recent situation that happened to help illustrate a beautiful way of resolving this...

Handling scope creep in the form of a "bug" being reported by your client...

It starts out innocently enough where the client thinks they've found a bug in the developer's code and asks them to help with a "quick fix".

Rob, the developer, just finished the project by saying:

> *Hey John,*
> *I have made the edits to this. Let me know*
> *if it looks right to you.*
> *Thanks!*

John, the client then replied back saying:

> *Hi Rob, great job. Is there a quick fix to*
> *edit the quantity box front-end so when*
> *this is changed the price is automatically*
> *updated?*

Then the developer replied back saying:

Hey John,

I took a quick look to see, but it looks like the quantity field update might be a bug in the plugin OR a little more than a quick fix. I would be happy to investigate it further if you wanted to come to an agreement for an additional task since it would be out of the scope of the current project we just finished. Or you might consider reaching out to the plugin author first. Just let me know.

Thanks!

Now on the surface, it looks great and is very professional and polite, but let's take a moment to break it down so you can understand what Rob is saying here.

Hopefully, it'll help YOU with preventing scope creep on projects you're involved with as well...

I took a quick look to see, but it looks like the quantity field update might be a bug in the plugin OR a little more than a quick fix.... you might consider reaching out to the plugin author first.

Notice Rob **didn't** tell the client right away <u>this is</u> <u>outside of the scope of work and I'm sorry but I can't</u> <u>help you with this unless you pay me more money.</u>

Rob took the time to actually look into it first and he saw where it may be a bug in the plugin, so he's providing value to the client in both looking into it briefly AND informing the client he may wish to consider going directly to the plugin author to have them fix it.

He's also managing the client's expectations that this really isn't a "quick fix" and will take time to look into so he's not able to make 2 clicks and have it solved.

Rob also says:

> *I would be happy to investigate it further if*
> *you wanted to come to an agreement for an*
> *additional task since it would be out of the*
> *scope of the current project we just finished.*

This is a great line because Rob isn't just telling the client, *'Sorry, I can't help you as it's out of scope and this is what we agreed to over here'...* He's instead telling him, *'Yes, I can look into this further for you to still try and help you'.*

Rob is also politely reminding the client the current project is finished but not in an in-your-face way.

Rob then places the ball in the client's court saying *'if you're interested, let me know and we'll talk more about this'.*

If the client decides to proceed, then Rob might consider using the troubleshooting method of pricing a project (like what is discussed in Chapter 6).

Remember to remain polite, be patient and helpful, and offer further assistance when needed.

Chapter Ten

Documenting Client's Projects

This is one of my favorite strategies because it takes a little bit of time, so few developers do it, and can have a big payout when executed.

Every time you work on a client's project, you should be documenting all details about the project in a spreadsheet. This includes:

- the client's name...

- their contact method (ie email address, Skype handle, etc...)

- the website...

- what theme is activated...

- what plugins are being used...

- what version of PHP they are running...

- what version of WP is installed...

Then subscribe to those theme and plugin mailing lists so you can be notified when a new release is launched. To not flood your inbox, you might consider creating a new email address or setting up some mailbox rules so that they auto-filter into a dedicated folder and don't just stay in your inbox. Also, be sure to closely monitor different WordPress vulnerability websites to stay informed of which plugins and themes have recent security vulnerabilities. A couple good sites to monitor is WPScan and SolidWP Vulnerability Report.

When a new update is released, or a new vulnerability is discovered, you can then message the client who has this particular software installed on their website and inform them of the new release (even better when it's a major release) asking if they would like assistance with safely updating their website using WordPress best-practices (making a backup of the live site and performing the updates on a staging environment first, of course).

You can let the client know what steps you'll take to ensure there is no downtime for the client's live website and that you'll be updating carefully and checking the staging environment to ensure nothing has broken. Then allow the client to check the staging site to also confirm everything looks great before pushing those changes to their live website.

I would also suggest letting your client understand the risks associated with NOT updating their theme, plugins, WP core, or PHP. You can even go so far as to remind them of the Panama Papers leak that was the result of an outdated version of Revolution Slider and the harm it caused to their business and their clients and that you don't want them to be exposed to the same kind of risk.

Then offer them a price to safely update their plug-ins, theme, WP core, or PHP version.

If you're concerned about the price and what if something breaks that takes additional time to repair, them simply let your client know that your price is for the updates and assuming nothing will break on the staging environment. However, if something does break, or a conflict is discovered, you'll let them know what is broken and provide another price to resolve the specific issues.

With the WordPress eco-system in a constant state of change and updates happening multiple times per year, you are offering an invaluable service to your clients by keeping on top of this for them.

By subscribing to all of the different themes and plugins' mailing lists, when a new update is being released or vulnerability discovered, you can do a <u>Find</u> in your spreadsheet of clients and see who is using that software. Then you'll know exactly who to reach out to about the update.

Many WordPress websites don't have a dedicated developer to maintain and monitor their systems, so having you as this resource is incredibly valuable and costs considerably less than if they were to hire someone full time to maintain their website.

Another option is to ask your client to set them up on a monthly retainer for a fixed fee to continually check on these types of issues and provide these safe updates for them as they are released. This leads to another income stream that we'll discuss in more detail in Chapter 13, Charging Clients For Monthly Retainers...

Chapter Eleven

How To Successfully Deliver A Project

Have you ever finished a project for a client, only to have the client ghost you and disappear, "forgetting" to mark it complete or paying you the remaining 50%?

This can be a frustrating experience, especially when you've worked so hard and put in the extra hours to have it ready in time for the client's 'urgent' deadline.

Here's a terrific way of delivering projects that makes you the *WP Dev Hero* and results in the client signing off and feeling good about the completion, in 7 simple steps...

1. Telling the client the work is now complete

Even the best developers can sometimes forget to actually tell the client the work is done. Maybe they finished working on it and assumed that the client knew based on a previously asked question or previously asking the client to review. But you shouldn't assume anything. Clients need to be told and it begins with politely informing the client the work is now done.

2. Explaining what work was carried out for the client

This is re-stating the Scope of Work that was originally agreed to, and reminding the client, everything really is now complete. It also reminds them of what areas to review so that they can confirm what has been done. And as a bonus, this helps to protect against scope creep!

3. Inform the client what browsers/devices the site and work was tested on

This not only tells the client what specific browsers and devices you tested the work on, but also that you DID test it!

Clients are taking a chance working with you and they're hoping (and sometimes praying) for a great experience. They want you to take the extra time to test everything before it's delivered, especially when they're paying a premium rate to work with you.

There's nothing worse than delivering a project and asking the client to test and they find all sorts of errors and issues. This can hurt your credibility and it shouldn't be left to them to test - you need to be doing QA on every project that has your name on it. It's your name, sign it with pride.

(Of course, be charging for this additional QA time by having it factored into your price you originally agreed on.)

4. Explain what the next step is for the client - if they're happy then to consider this is complete (or mark it complete) and how to pay the other 50%

This is key! Remember, you need to be telling the client what the next step is and don't assume they know to mark something as complete or that they need to pay you the remaining fee for completing the work and before it's delivered to their live site.

5. Thanking the client and reminding them you're still here for them, even after delivery.

This is very rare and not many developers outside of Codeable do this. But this is what helps to separate you from the rest of the developers and makes you a real *WP Dev Hero* and in *The Top 2%*.

Clients can be afraid that when they indicate a project is complete and pay you the remaining fee today (or mark a project complete on a platform), that they'll discover something is wrong tomorrow and they'll be left high and dry and you'll be gone forever, along with their money.

Letting the client know you're still here for them helps them feel comfortable with considering it complete. Some developers even go so far as offering a limited warranty on bugs found with their code. Decide how long you feel comfortable, but a good rule of thumb, is the longer the better. Codeable offers an industry leading 28 day warranty and it's very rare that a client ever makes use of it.

This can further separate you from the sea of other developers online by standing behind your work. If you offer a warranty period, make sure to let the client know what it is and how many days you'll cover for bugs found.

6. Adding A Short Tutorial Video To Their Admin

I was on a call with a brilliant developer recently who told me a wonderful tactic that he was using and having massive success with. In order to help the client <u>and</u> deliver additional value, he would record a short video walkthrough of how to use their new WordPress website that he just created for them.

He would record his screen taking the client through what each main part of the admin was:

- how to add new pages and posts...

- how to upload images...

- how to save drafts and publish pages...

- the basics of how to use their page builder (if used), etc..

He would overlay his name and logo at the bottom of the video and then attach it to the client's WP Admin dashboard so that it would appear every time they would log into their site. As a result, the client ends up seeing his picture and logo every time they log in and most clients do watch it at least once.

The beauty of this is 2-fold.

One, the client sees your name, logo and your face every time they log-in to their website, further anchoring your "brand" recognition. This helps to keep you top of mind for any future work the client may be wanting to proceed with.

Two, it prevents the clients from messaging you in the future asking how to perform simple tasks.

Again, this wasn't a long video, often only 5 minutes or less in total run time, but the payoff is huge. Clients will know exactly who to contact for additional work, and who better to work on it than the person who built it.

7. Letting the client know how to work with you in the future on another project

This may be more applicable if you're working with a client on a platform or marketplace, but it can still apply to working with a direct client that you've found yourself.

If it's a client you've found yourself, then perhaps you've set the client up with a special Slack channel for the project you've just finished up and it'll be easier for the client and you to communicate via this Slack channel for future work. If this is the case, make sure to inform the client of this, that it'll be best/easiest or that they can receive the fastest assistance by pinging you directly in this Slack channel if there's any future work they might need help with.

If this is a client you've found on a marketplace, like UpWork, Freelancer or Codeable, then this is explaining to the client how they can easily work with you again on the platform. You'll want to build up a nice group of repeat clients who specifically request to work with you every time - on every request!

The goal is to get you so many awesome repeat clients specifically reaching out to YOU that you never have to go searching for new clients. At least not actively searching on a continuous basis. They all come directly to you. And this is further ensured by following the steps laid out in Chapter 10, Documenting Client's Projects and Chapter 14, Sending Holiday Messages.

As good as this delivery is, there's a way to take it to the next level. Something again *The Top 2%* do... the art of up-sells and down-sells.

Chapter Twelve

Up-Sells And Down-Sells

This is a fantastic way to maximize your revenue per project and client. The idea here is that when you're finished with the client's project, to then offer suggestions and recommendations for additional work that you feel would be of benefit to the client and their website.

Let's imagine you go to the doctor to get treatment for removing a wart. While the doctor is removing the wart, he notices a mole on your arm that looks suspicious and is concerned it may be cancerous. Would you want the doctor to tell you about this suspect mole and offer to treat it? Of course you would! After all, this could save your life.

Being in *The Top 2%*, a true *WP Dev Hero*, means you should start thinking of yourself as a doctor and bringing things to a client's attention that you feel are important.

When you're working on a client's website, you're in the backend of their system, you're looking at their WP Admin. You're seeing all of the out-dated plugins, theme, WP Core, and PHP. You're noticing the many deactivated, but still installed (and likely outdated) plugins and themes. You're seeing how their website contains various security vulnerabilities and is placing their site, their business, and their visitors/clients at risk. You're noticing the load times of the client's website. You're seeing where the client is attempting to collect leads on their site, but missing several opportunities to get even more leads by using something like the Hello Bar or an exit-pop. You're noticing the client is placing zero effort on SEO, does not have an SEO plugin installed, and none of the content on the site is optimized.

It's in the client's best interest to have these concerns brought to their attention, just like a doctor informing you of a suspicious looking mole.

After your main project together is complete, inform the client about their outdated theme, plugins, or WP core. Then explain why this is dangerous and when possible, cite references from credible sources, like this Forbes article, that states over 30,000 websites get hacked every day. And how one of the ways hackers gain access to a website is through outdated themes, plugins, and WP core.

Then offer your assistance with resolving these issues for them.

Be sure to mention that normally for new clients/projects, that this would cost $XXX. BUT since you've been working on their website, you already know what needs to be done, the staging environment is already created, and the ramp-up time is much less compared to working with someone new. Therefore you'll be able to complete these updates for them for only $YYY. (meaning giving them a slight discount since they won't need to pay for the ramp-up of a new developer or staging environment).

The client just had a great experience working with you, they already trust you, and depending on the issue you bring to their attention, they won't want to place their business at risk or cause any downtime to their business by not addressing this.

Not to mention the added cost to clean up a hacked website and patch any backdoors that get created is considerably more than applying the updates to their site before it's hacked.

The same applies to any of the other options I mentioned above.

For example, if their website is taking 13 seconds to load, then offer them a speed optimization task letting them know about Amazon stating that for every 1 second additional it takes to load their website, they lose $1.5 billion. And that a slow website is costing them money.

If the client is running PPC or paid ads to their website, and it's taking too long to load, then people are clicking Back and they are wasting ad-spend because they paid for that click. So not only is it costing a client sales to have a slow loading site, it's costing them money on wasted ads where visitors don't even land on their site.

Then further detail the issue and back up your statement by sharing a GTMetrix or Pingdom (or both) speed test report and letting them see for themselves how long it takes for their site to load.

Sometimes a client will kind of know their site is taking a "little while" to load, but they've never run any tests or timed it to see just how long it's taking. So by showing them the actual stats, it will back up your claim and give them evidence of their slow loading site.

Then offer them a speed optimization package that will get their site loading faster. Be careful when managing expectations and not to over-promise and under-deliver as that will also leave a bad impression with the client.

Not only can you get another up-sell on the speed task, but if you ultimately end up migrating the client to a new hosting company (which can lead to an almost instant improvement in speed by moving them away from a budget host), then there's additional compensation (commission) if you're an affiliate of the recommended new host. So you might be able to add an additional $200 commission payment on top of the $1,000 ı speed task.

So long as you have the client's best interest in mind, there should be no question of your motives or ethics involved. I'll talk a bit more about affiliate commissions in Chapter 16, but this is another fantastic way to increase your revenue per project.

It's also really classy to inform the client that you're sharing an affiliate link with them, and that while you may earn a small commission for the referral, you are recommending this because it's the best solution for the client and that you have their best interests in mind.

Now, what's this thing called a down-sell and how can you start utilizing these?

If a client you're engaging with isn't interested in your up-sell (like the speed optimization task), chances are they can't afford it (at this time).

So instead of telling the client, *"Ok, I understand, well let me know when you might be ready and I'll be here for you..."*

You can be pro-active and offer a down-sell of a smaller speed task. Chances are they already understand the benefit of having a faster website because you already shared some info and stats and showed them how slow their current website is.

So instead of doing a full-blown speed optimization where you can get them to a 1-2 second load time, you can offer a reduced speed optimization project that might get them to a 4 second load time.

It's less work for you as the developer, the client still receives value from you and gets a faster website, and you're helping to fill your capacity and earning more revenue. Everyone is still winning here.

Always offer the higher price packages first, and if the client can't afford the service but recognizes the need, then offer a reduced scope of work that still gives them value. And with the migration to a new host, you'll be earning the additional commission and ultimately be earning more money on the project.

The same goes for a security package. If you normally charge $500 for a full security package, and the client can't afford it right now, then offer a lower-priced version. Maybe it only includes a couple of bigger vulnerabilities, like updating all of their plugins, theme, and core. Maybe it also includes the installation of a free plugin like WordFence or SolidWP.

Or maybe you could talk them into changing to a more secure hosting company where you'll again earn an additional affiliate commission for the referral. Explain the benefits of being with a more secure host, like WP Engine, and how they pro-actively protect the websites on their network and for only $200 you could help to safely migrate them. Then you'll be earning the $200 for the migration service, and another $200 commission from WP Engine, and as a bonus, their site speed will likely improve, so they'll be receiving even more value.

When you're showing your client just how valuable you are, they'll continue to want to work with you for years to come. You're their trusted partner for anything web-related.. you're their doctor they go to when they need help and whom they rely on to be pro-active and spot issues before they turn into nightmares.

Coupling this with our other strategies outlined, like Chapter 14 on Sending Holiday Messages and Chapter 10, documenting their tech stack to notify them when major releases of their theme and plugins (or core) are pushed out, you'll be sitting in a very good, very safe, very predictable income stream.

Chapter Thirteen

Charging Clients For Monthly Retainers

(Or Monthly Maintenance Fees)

R etainers are a fantastic way to help your clients and provide stable predictable revenue for your freelancing business.

As I mentioned previously, the WordPress eco-system is in a constant state of change with updates happening multiple times per year. You are in a perfect position to offer an invaluable service to your clients by keeping on top of this for them.

Many WordPress websites don't have a dedicated developer to maintain and monitor their systems, so having you as this resource is incredibly valuable and

costs considerably less than if they were to hire someone full time to maintain their website.

Some ideas to consider when offering clients
monthly retainers are:

- Offering a set number of development hours
  per month to handle requests that come up
  (with additional hours being billed on top of
  the retainer)

- Offering them a dedicated WordPress specialist to help them (which is you!)

- Offering priority emergency care (for when
  the unexpected should arise)

- Offering offsite backups

- Offering updates to their theme, plugins, and
  core

- Offering malware and virus scanning

- Offering uptime monitoring

- Offering to post X number of blog posts
  (which they supply the content for) each

month, including basic SEO optimization of each article

- Offering to help them craft marketing emails to send (using their content) and scheduling it each week

- Offering additional services you feel would be helpful for your client based on their needs

There are lots of different ways to package your retainers and there may not be a "1 solution fits all approach", so it is often best to talk with your client to see which services they are interested in and then customize the retainer just for them.

I know of a WP developer that has 12 clients all on retainers varying in size from $100 per month up to $4500 per month and everything in between. These retainers alone account for over $8,000 in monthly revenue that is predictable, stable, and a very nice income stream that they can rely on month after month.

Having this predictable income stream reduces much of the stress associated with freelance work so that you no longer need to worry about your (monthly) house payment, food, internet, kid's schooling, etc. as it's already covered every month. This can help you sleep easier and prevent your hair from turning grey (or falling out) due to worry and fear of where the next project will be coming from.

If you don't offer your client a retainer, they'll likely never ask you for it. **So start asking** and start setting these up for your clients. They'll be thanking you for helping them and being their Go-To WP developer for all their needs.

This will actually help your clients from feeling stressed out and worried about their website crashing or being vulnerable. So again it's a win-win situation for both parties involved.

When working with a client on a retainer basis, you'll want to be careful to over-communicate with your client every month (and ideally every week).

Even with good solid relationships, it can become easy for your client to get concerned that you're not actually working for their money and watching episodes on Netflix instead of working on their website. After all, if their site isn't having any issues, then where is the time going every month?

To prevent this from becoming an issue, I suggest posting weekly status updates (preferably on Fridays) detailing what work was done for the week. Then stating what work is being planned for the next week. If you're tracking your hours using a time-tracker tool, then also post the details of those working hours that are being logged and recorded.

And if possible, it would be great for you to schedule weekly check-in calls with your client to get them on the phone, let them hear your voice, and re-stating the work that was done for the previous week, along with what work is being planned for the following week, and ask them if they have any questions.

This will really separate the amateurs from the professionals and show them you're a true *WP Dev Hero*. It's very professional and allowing them to hear your voice can go a long way in keeping their trust high so that the retainer will continue on for many months and even years into the future.

As I mentioned before, the first client I ever got (my new "dad" friend down the street who owned the restaurant), paid me on a retainer basis $400 per month, for over 2 years. I kept an eye on his site, had scheduled backups being made, uptime monitoring, and would help him with random tasks and requests he had. I was careful with my time, tracking how much time I was spending each month, and kept in regular communication with him.

There are so many millions of WordPress websites in the world, 1,000s in your local area alone. It shouldn't be any problem finding 10 who are seeing your value and willing to pay you $400 monthly.

A secret tip for you... agencies make the best retainer clients. It's very possible that you can land 1 agency client and explain how your retainers work, how they benefit the agency owner, and how it benefits their clients, and quickly have 4-6 retainers going each month, just for this single agency; one for each of the agency's own clients.

Often, the agency will not have thought of offering their clients retainers. So you'll have planted the seed about how this is a valuable resource and service you're providing. Then you'll have also created a new revenue stream for the agency; where you might be charging the agency $400 per month per site, and then can turn around and charge $800 per month per site to their clients. So the agency (your client) is thrilled and excited, and this one person can get you multiple sites signed up on retainers.

You might be asking, well that's great, but how can I get in front of agency clients?

Agencies need dev services too. Just because they have in-house developers, they may need help on some WooCommerce extension that they don't have the skillset to handle, but you do. Or they don't have the Gravity Forms knowledge that you do and they need to outsource part of a client's project to you...

Consider Googling the name of each one of your clients to learn more about them, where they work, what their role is, etc. It's possible you've already worked with an agency and didn't even realize it.

It doesn't matter how the agency client gets in front of you, you should always explain at the end of the successful project together, that you offer retainer services to clients, and how some of your happiest clients have been agencies, and this is what the service looks like...

The only way you'll sell clients on retainers is by asking. If you don't ask, the client may not either.

Chapter Fourteen

Sending Holiday Messages To Clients

This sounds basic and simple, but it's often these "simple" tactics that work the best. Implement this consistently and it can have a big impact.

I've heard from several high earning *(Hero)* developers who said that they take a few moments to message ALL of the existing clients they've ever worked with to wish them a happy holidays; whether it's to say Happy Easter, Happy Hanukkah, Merry Christmas, Happy New Years, Happy Valentine's Day, Happy Thanksgiving, etc., there are a number of major holidays throughout the year and these developers who take a few moments to wish their client a heartfelt holiday, they often get 4-6 new projects as a result.

There's no selling involved in these messages and don't confuse this for a sales opportunity as that won't have the same desired impact.

Keep the message short and sweet and use it as an opportunity to just say Hi and let them know you were thinking of them and wishing them happy holidays.

Clients appreciate the heartfelt sentiment and as an added bonus, it reminds them you exist. It also can remind them that they do need some development work done and since they had a great experience with you previously, who better to ask for help on their new request?

A specific developer I spoke with said that this tactic consistently results in him landing several $300-600 projects and 1 new larger project, like a site re-design valued at several thousand dollars. Not bad for a few messages sent out. And this consistently happens every time he sends out his holiday messages.

So many developers don't take the time to ever reach back out to past clients. They are instead always on the hunt for new clients, often forgetting about the old.

Don't under-estimate the value of a relationship and taking a few moments to send out holiday messages. This really can have a large impact on your revenue if you'll do it. Will you be a *WP Dev Hero* in *The Top 2%* and message clients for the holidays?

Chapter Fifteen

Manufacturing Celebrity

*"You get paid more for WHO you are,
than for WHAT you do..."*

I've heard this many times from one of the greatest direct response marketers and copyrighters, Dan Kennedy.

There are several ways that you can manufacture celebrity and command higher rates.

These include writing a book, guest posting on other websites, giving talks at different events, hosting your own Meetup, being a guest on different podcasts, hosting your own podcast, and posting videos on social platforms like TikTok, Facebook Live, YouTube Live and Shorts, and Instagram Stories, just to name a few.

I believe there are a couple of primary ways to manufacture celebrity and in my opinion, writing a book and building your social media presence / audience are two great ways to establish yourself as an expert. Both of these can open doors for you that might otherwise remain closed.

When you're an author and/or influencer, you instantly become more credible. This can then lead to many other opportunities; whether that's speaking on a stage, guest posting on other sites, being a guest on podcasts... everything becomes a bit easier when you have this additional credibility.

Perhaps it's not an either/or situation, but rather an "and" situation. Meaning you have time to accomplish both; be an influencer AND an author.

When thinking about writing a book, you no longer need to write a book and send it to publishers and hope one of them will offer to place you under their umbrella. There are many self-publication options available, such as Amazon KDP, Lulu, IngramSpark, and more.

Your book likely won't make you rich from the direct sales of it (often published book authors earn $1-2 for each copy sold or $5-10 if you self-publish). But don't let this discourage you in the slightest because the money is made on the backend of writing the book.

Meaning, people inherently pay more attention to and give more respect to someone who has written a book. And inside of the book, you can link back to your website for additional resources (perhaps a lead magnet such as a free report or cheatsheet), or to instruct readers on how to work with you directly.

Pro Tip: Elevate your freelance development career by connecting with like-minded devs in The Top 2%. At Skool.com/freelance-dev-hero, not only will you gain exclusive access to a community of elite developers, but you'll also receive several white-labeled lead magnets. Customize these valuable resources with your own branding and use them to capture potential clients' contact

> information effortlessly. Don't miss this chance to enhance your network and resource toolkit—join us today and start transforming your freelance journey

Your book can also help you with getting speaking engagements, becoming a guest on a podcast, guest blogging, or even working with new clients.

When you meet a prospective new client, instead of handing them your business card, you can hand them your book. They certainly won't toss it aside or lose it in between the seat of their car like they might a business card. Even if they don't read it, they'll see that you're different from all the other developers they meet (and who certainly don't have a book) and it'll provide you with more credibility and authority because of it. As an added bonus, this can also help you to command higher rates.

If you're interested in writing a book, Another great option is to use a website like HelpAReporter.com You can register on this website and get contacted any time a reporter needs a credible expert to interview.

This can lead to news coverage, both in print and on TV, which will then allow you to use the logo of the news outlet that featured you, thereby adding to your "celebrity" status. And this will also help if you have a book and the reporter knows you're a more credible resource than Joe down the street.

You might also consider applying to talk at Word-Camp events in your area. If/when you are recorded and placed on WordCamp.tv, you can then link to your talk and again include this logo in your website and it again positions you more like a celebrity.

Try reaching out to site editors about guest blogging, especially on larger sites, like Huffington Post, WSJ, Forbes, Wired, etc. Many developers are granted this privilege and again if you submit your proposed article along with a link to your book for sale on Amazon, it helps lend additional credibility to you. When you get this guest post published, you'll then be able to link back to your article and feature the logo on your own website and in your email footer.

Don't be shy and reach out to podcasters and offer them a copy of your book and offer yourself for interviews. Podcasters are always looking for new content and people to interview. This is your chance to get in front of their audience (which by the way, people who listen to podcasts earn on average $80,00-100,000 per year), and the podcast episode stays online for years. So by doing a single podcast, you can get leads and clients requesting your help for a really long time.

Don't just do 1 interview, try and line up 1 interview every month. This will have a compounding effect and those 12 per year will continue generating new leads for you. Hopefully, I don't need to keep mentioning it, but having your own book will help you land more guest spots here too!

If you'd like to consider writing a book, there's a great book to help show you how called "How To Write a Book This Weekend, Even If You Flunked English Like I Did" by Vic Johnson. I read this one and found it very helpful and useful.

Then another book I highly recommend is called "Book The Business: How To Make BIG MONEY With Your Book Without Even Selling A Single Copy" by Adam Witty and Dan Kennedy.

The first book will help you to get your own book written fast. If you think there's no way you can ever write a book in a weekend, it's actually entirely possible and just requires the decision and determination to do it.

TL;DR, Vic Johnson recommends making an outline of the topics you'll cover in your book (which will later become your chapters), then using an audio recorder to record yourself talking about each chapter. Then you can send that audio file to have it transcribed or use an AI tool. Afterwards, send the transcription over to an editor to have it cleaned up. He goes into more detail in the book, but just know, it's a lot easier than you think.

And then the Dan Kennedy book will guide you in-depth on how to use your book to position yourself as an expert. Watch doors open easier and faster than you ever thought possible, all by authoring your own book.

When pursuing the path to becoming an influencer, the key is to just start. In other words, press record and just go for it.

In my opinion, one of the largest hurdles to overcome is the mental-side of "putting yourself out there".

Worrying about what others may think of you... worrying people will criticize you... worrying about people leaving negative comments...

These are all enough to keep people from achieving their greatness. However, if you focus on who your ideal customer is (who you want to help), you can begin creating content for that group. Then with this in-mind, just press record and know your first 20 videos will likely be terrible. And that's OK.

At the time of writing this, MrBeast, is the largest YouTuber with the largest social media following in the world. And while he has hundred of millions of followers on YouTube alone (let alone his follower count on TikTok, Instagram, Facebook, X, and others) I recommend watching a few of his oldest videos on YouTube; where he got his start, to realize nobody is born charismatic and comfortable on-screen.

MrBeast's videos in the beginning primarily featured him playing Minecraft, Pokemon, BlackOps, and a couple other games while narrating them in post-production (meaning after he recorded them), then uploading them to YouTube. It took him around 110 videos and 2 years before he ever showed his face.

But he stuck with it and he didn't give up. He took it more seriously and began researching other successful creators, their videos, their thumbnails, their pacing and more. Until he finally got more comfortable on camera and understood what made a view-worthy video. A video people actually wanted to watch.

Moral of the story?

Don't give up and just press record. Understand who you want to help (your ideal client) and just make videos for them.

All of this is helping to establish yourself like a Celebrity and therefore command higher prices for the services you offer.

So then it's a matter of positioning yourself as the expert, the celebrity, and showing off your accolades.

When you do end up posting guest blog articles on sites, or being on a podcast, or speaking at a Word-Camp, be sure place these brand logos on your website, in your email footer, your social media profiles, your business card, and anywhere else you can think of or where it makes sense. This is helping you to brand yourself and you're creating your own celebrity status.

Remember, you get paid more for Who you are, than for What you do.

Chapter Sixteen

Affiliate Deals

This is a great way to earn more money while working as a freelance developer. You likely already know about affiliate commissions, but just in case you aren't familiar, this is when you offer a product or service to a client, and if the client buys through your special affiliate link, you'll earn a commission for the recommendation.

Before we continue, I'm going to assume that you'll always act in a professional ethical (Hero) manner and only recommend products and services to clients when there is truly a reason to do so. That said, I won't continue making this disclaimer and will just continue...

There are many products and services that have affiliate programs, and I'll suggest signing up for several so that you'll be ready for when the time comes to make recommendations to clients.

Think about it this way... if a doctor refers you to see a specialist for X-Rays, or writes you a prescription, then you'll do as the doctor instructs you, right? Well it's very likely that doctor will earn a referral fee from either the X-Ray business or the Pharmaceutical company who makes the drugs, each time they make a recommendation for you and you follow through with it.

You should be ready to write your own prescriptions as well.

Prescriptions for a slow loading site; this might be for a new hosting company or for WP Rocket. A prescription for a vulnerable site; maybe a paid plugin or Sucuri protection. A prescription for themes; like StudioPress or Divi. A prescription for increasing WooCommerce sales; using a tool like CartFlows. A prescription for collecting leads; like an autoresponder such as ConvertKit. You get the idea...

Start with making a list of all the tools you regularly use for clients and already recommend, and check to see if they have an affiliate program. Most do and their payouts can range from a few dollars to a few hundred dollars, and some are recurring payouts each time the client renews their subscription with the company.

I know some WP Dev Heroes in the Top 2% who perform 3-4 speed optimization tasks per month for clients, and ultimately recommend migrating to a new host for the best possible performance. This results in an additional $600-800 per month in affiliate commissions; commissions that would have otherwise been left on the table (and out of the developer's pocket) had they not been an affiliate. This is extra revenue and income on top of the money they charge to perform the migration or perform the speed optimization.

Please make sure to always make ethical recommendations and do not recommend products or services which don't truly benefit your client. By keeping your client's needs top priority, you'll stay out of trouble and sleep better at night.

When completing a client's request involves the purchase of any themes or plugins, it's best to have the client purchase the software on their own (and using your affiliate link). When your client purchases it in their own name and email, then they can receive the updates and support themselves. Then after purchase, ask the client to share the download or account details so you can download and install/configure the software for them.

> *Pro Tip: Use a link shortener or install the Pretty Links plugin to provide your client with a nicer looking link to click on versus a long and sometimes "ugly" affiliate link.*

This is a really valuable service to the client, and also you're getting compensated for the referral, so it's really a win-win for everyone involved.

As I mentioned earlier, it's really classy to inform the client that you're sharing an affiliate link with them, and that while you may earn a small commission for the referral, you are recommending this because it's the best solution for the client and that you have their best interests in mind. Also that it won't cost them anything extra for clicking through your link and in some cases, may even provide them with an additional discount they otherwise wouldn't receive. So it's a win-win.

Chapter Seventeen

How To Structure Your Working Environment To Be More Productive And Lower Stress

W here and how you work is very important to your overall stress, productivity, and efficiency.

I was recently speaking with a terrific, brilliant developer, who told me he was feeling stressed lately.

When asked why, he responded saying he feels like he's always on-call for his clients.

That he found himself always working on his laptop on the sofa, even though he had a desktop machine in the other room. The problem was he didn't find the chair at the desk comfortable and so it was just more convenient and more comfortable working from the sofa with the laptop in his lap.

He also mentioned that he would be watching TV at night with his significant other and could never seem to relax. He always felt the need to be checking in on emails and notifications from clients at all hours of the night.

This was causing major stress in his life and having a negative impact on his relationship because he would hear the *ding* of his computer alerting him of an incoming message and he felt the need to check to see what it was... much to the disappointment of his significant other.

The problem was, he had conditioned himself to always be working on the sofa, and so to him, he was associating (subconsciously) that the sofa = work.

He'd hear the notification of a new incoming message and would think of work. He would think of the client on the other end of that notification and how they are so accustomed to receiving an immediate response, that if he didn't respond, he may lose the client or they would become upset because they're having an emergency and he's not available to help.

I suggested he stop working immediately from the sofa and to get himself a new comfortable chair for his desk. Also that he should inform all of his clients of his new "Office Hours" and that if they message him outside of those hours, then he'll reply back as soon as he gets online the following business day. And if he is worried about client's having an emergency situation, that they could message him via Skype, but only in emergencies, and that there is an after-hours surcharge that gets applied to all requests made after-hours.

My developer friend liked these suggestions and decided to test them.

He bought himself a nice new office desk chair that was really comfortable. He began using his dual-monitor desktop computer again. He informed all of his clients of his new office hours and of the after-hours surcharge that will be applied for emergency requests.

I reconnected with him after 2 weeks and he was thrilled to let me know of the transformation!

He said his stress levels have gone down tremendously. He no longer feels like he's always working and makes it a point to not work from the sofa any longer.

He also told me about how his productivity and efficiency working on client's projects has gone through the roof! He said he's getting so much more done now because of the 2 monitors and full-size keyboard and mouse. So now he's completing more work in less time (and as a result, he's earning more money).

He also told me that his relationship with his significant other has improved and how much she appreciates having him all to herself now without him constantly checking in on work. They are reconnecting and spending more quality time together.

He also mentioned that clients are overwhelmingly accepting of his new office hours and he's only had a single person complain about it; and that he never really liked that client anyway and so he stopped working with him — which further reduced his stress levels.

All areas of his freelance developer life have improved––all from making a few minor adjustments to how he was working.

He said now he's looking at buying an adjustable-height standing desk so he can try to stay healthier while working.

I'd like to suggest you take a look at how you're working...

Are you working from the sofa or recliner most days?

Do you feel like you're always on-call with your clients and feel the stress of needing to reply back asap at all hours of the day and weekend?

Do you have a desk with dual monitors that you could be using, but maybe you don't like the size/height of your desk or is your chair uncomfortable?

There are some great articles online recommending the proper desk height so that your posture and body position are optimal and that keeps your (blood) circulation flowing properly.

Don't forget to stand up every hour. Take a few deep breathes, get yourself a fresh glass of water or a healthy snack from the kitchen (I personally love almonds), and even better if you can take a few steps outside to gaze out onto the horizon and breathe some fresh air.

You might also look into investing in a pair of blue-light blocking glasses to help reduce eye strain and fatigue. It's good to look away from the screen every 10-20 minutes, even for just a moment, so that your eyes can relax and not be so strained extended periods of time.

Standing desks are a great investment and so are walking desks if you have space and budget for them. I've also seen cycling desks so you can pedal while you work.

Breathing exercises and yoga are amazing as well and I can't recommend them enough. It's the little things that can make a big difference in your life.

I encourage you to look at making some of these small changes in your working environment and I hope you can find more happiness and less stress while freelancing.

Stay healthy, keep stress to a minimum, and have fun while you work.

Medical disclaimer: Please consult your physician or health care provider before starting any exercise routines and know that I'm not a doctor, just a friend who's passionate about helping freelance WordPress developers.

Chapter Eighteen

Take Care Of Your Mental Well-Being

While working as a freelance WordPress developer, it can be stressful. Clients aren't always the easiest people to get along with and sometimes no matter how hard you try to make someone happy, it's just not possible.

You need to learn that you can't make all the people happy all the time. Even if you do everything right, deliver when you say you will, it's possible the client will be upset over something. Even if it's not your fault and even if the client is upset because you won't do additional out of scope work for free.

So try not to let it affect you and don't stress over it and dwell on it.

Like Richard Carlson says and writes about, *"Don't Sweat the Small Stuff... and it's all small stuff."*

I'm aware this is easier said than done. I've personally allowed myself to get too caught up working with clients and sometimes they really know how to push your buttons.

But even if the client is not acting professional, please try to always remain professional yourself. You might use the Abraham Lincoln method of writing a letter (or opening a notepad doc these days). Proceed to tell the client how you really feel. Really let them have it and be as harsh and nasty as you want! Get it all out of your system and on to paper (or the computer).

Then do <u>NOT</u> send it!

Take a break from the computer, go for a walk outside, get some food and freshen your drink.

Then when you get back in front of the computer, compose a professional email reply and leave out all of the "stuff" that will escalate the situation.

In the end, if you need to refund the client and walk away, do that. Get that stress and toxic client out of your life and just be done and move on. There are always more clients out there and when you're not dealing with the jerks, it leaves you open to work with other nicer clients who value and respect you more.

Also, don't be afraid to say *"No"* every once in a while. If you have a client who is always rude or unprofessional, tell the client "No" when they ask you for more work. This again can free you up to work with other nicer clients.

I've heard from several developer friends who said they finally cut out a toxic client, and then a few days later, a nice returning client messaged them asking for help on a larger multiple month long engagement. They were so happy they didn't have that toxic client any longer because otherwise they wouldn't have had the capacity to help the nice client on their new request. You'll be pleasantly surprised how the universe works like this.

I'd like to also mention that it's easy to get caught up in the work, work, work mindset.

Having a work-life balance is incredibly important for your mental health and well-being.

So what does work-life balance mean in the real world?

To me, personally, it means taking time to un-plug and do things that I enjoy and that fill me up.

For example, I love spending time with my wife and kids. I also love to wakeskate (it's like skateboarding, but on the water behind a boat or jetski) and not only is it fantastic exercise, but it's fun as all heck!

Every day I do my best to stop working at 5:30pm so that I can see my family, help with cooking dinner, assisting my kids with some homework, and playing outside together. Then after dinner, we have our bed-time routine where we say our prayers as a family, have a bit of story time, tuck them in bed, and turn off the lights.

Then I make it a point every night to spend quality time with my wife. Sometimes we watch a couple of episodes together on Netflix, and other times we sit on the couch and talk and stream Pandora for some background music (usually something high vibrational, like Enya lol).

This is super important and I'll tell you why...

A few years ago, my wife suggested that I not spend this time with her after laying the kids down for bed. She knows that after she goes to bed, I turn back on the computer and will typically work from around 9:30pm when she goes to bed, until 11-12am, every day. And so to help me get more rest at night, she would rather I work a few hours after laying the kids down so that I could go to sleep at a reasonable hour.

I was very appreciative of her love and support at this suggestion and so for a few months I was doing this.

However, while I was getting more rest and not working so late, our personal relationship was suffering. We began arguing more and really started losing our connection together.

It took me a little while to figure out this was a result of not spending this quality time each night to reconnect with each other.

She occasionally still recommends I do my work instead of spending time with her, and I always thank her for her love and support, but politely decline and choose to spend this time with her each evening.

As a result, I do tend to work a bit too late into the evening (always my own choice though) and our relationship is stronger than ever.

If you or someone you know is struggling with any personal issues, there's a fantastic resource specifically for the WordPress community, called Big Orange Heart.

You can find them at www.bigorangeheart.org

Big Orange Heart provides mental health support within the WordPress community and now more broadly the freelance community. And even though they're based in the U.K., they provide support all around the globe.

There's a dedicated Slack channel, a Facebook Group, and even local Meetups. You can also email them or call them anonymously if you're ever going through a hard time and need someone to talk to.

I really encourage you, please, reach out to them if you're needing help or contact a local mental health professional in your area.

Please don't look for a permanent solution to a temporary problem. Find someone you can talk to and know that you are loved and there are people who care about you and want to help you.

Chapter Nineteen

Conclusion

As you've noticed by now, there really aren't any earth-shattering tactics or strategies presented in this book. I'm also not asking you to trick anyone or do anything weird or unethical.

While these strategies are easy to do and to implement, they're also easy not to do.

It's easy to install and use Grammarly or Language-Tool or use chatGPT, but it's also easy to not use these tools.

It's easy to document a client's project, but it's also easy to keep doing what you're doing and leave all client's projects un-documented and scattered around your email, Skype, or WhatsApp apps.

It's easy to send a holiday message to all of your clients, but it's easy not to send out any holiday messages.

If you enjoy always being in a state of feast of famine as a freelance WordPress developer, then you might consider gifting this book to a friend of yours... someone who might take these lessons and chapters to heart and act on them.

But something tells me that's not the case. I have a strong feeling that you're looking for a change. That you're looking for things to get better. And for things to get better, you have to get better.

Take the time to implement each of these strategies, but also don't feel like you need to implement every single one of them immediately. Try just 1 or 2 at a time that make the most sense to you. And don't be afraid to try each one multiple times.

These strategies are not like a magic potion that will instantly cause every single client to pull out their wallet and hand you money. They are, however, infinitely more powerful and work much more often than leaving everything to chance and hoping your client will pay you more money and ask you for more work.

I strongly encourage you to keep track of your clients and which clients you offered up-sells to, which clients you sent holiday messages to, which clients you offered retainers to, etc.

Then later you can analyze the data and know your conversions of how many clients you asked about up-sells and how many took them; how many clients you sent holiday messages to and how many replied back asking you for more work; how many clients you offered retainers to and how many took them...

Then with this data, tweak the messages you're using and track conversions again. Keep A/B testing everything to find what works best for you.

Remember, even though you're a freelancer, you're still running a business. While you don't have a "boss" telling you what to do or how to do it, you want to hold yourself accountable.

And with that, I will end this book. Thank you so much for reading, and I wish you much success and happiness... and here's to becoming the *WP Dev Hero* you were destined to be.

Ready to elevate your skills and become a top 2% WordPress developer?

Join our community at Skool.com/freelance -dev-hero. Here, you'll find not just support and guidance, but a thriving network of peers who are eager to share their knowledge and experience.

Gain access to exclusive resources, get encouragement from fellow freelance devs, and harness collective wisdom to refine your craft. Don't navigate your development journey alone—become a Freelance Dev Hero and start transforming your career today.

Chapter Twenty

References

http://www.WPDevHero.com

https://www.skool.com/freelance-dev-hero

https://www.upwork.com

https://www.freelancer.com

https://www.guru.com

https://www.isvictorious.com/upwork-freelancing-guide

http://craigslist.org

https://www.reddit.com/r/forhire

https://codeable.io

https://www.facebook.com/JulieChristineStoian

https://www.facebook.com/groups/freedomhackersmastermind

https://www.facebook.com/groups/ftfpcommuni
ty

https://www.facebook.com/groups/dannyveigahu
stlegroup

https://www.facebook.com/groups/therisingtides
ociety

http://www.linkedin.com/groups/56766/profile

http://www.linkedin.com/groups/1789386/profil
e

http://www.linkedin.com/groups/39824/profile

http://www.linkedin.com/groups/62352/profile

https://belive.tv

https://www.moo.com/us/business-cards/luxe

https://www.mountaingoatsoftware.com/agile/us
er-stories

https://wpvulndb.com/

https://www.forbes.com/sites/jameslyne/2013/09
/06/30000-web-sites-hacked-a-day-how-do-you-host
-yours/#740eb3dc1738

https://wpengine.com

https://www.amazon.com/Write-Book-Weekend
-Flunked-English-ebook/dp/B00BZBWWQS

https://www.amazon.com/Book-Business-Withou
t-Selling-Single/dp/1599324075

https://www.bigorangeheart.org